Hors d'Oeuvres & Appetizers

GENERAL EDITOR
CHUCK WILLIAMS

RECIPES
THE SCOTTO SISTERS

PHOTOGRAPHY
ALLAN ROSENBERG

TIME
LIFE
BOOKS

Time-Life Books

is a division of TIME LIFE INC.,
a wholly owned subsidiary of
THE TIME INC. BOOK COMPANY

President: John M. Fahey

TIME-LIFE BOOKS

President: Mary Davis
Publisher: Robert H. Smith
Vice President and Associate Publisher:
  Trevor Lunn
Vice President and Associate Publisher:
  Susan J. Maruyama
Director of Special Markets: Frances C. Mangan
Marketing Director: Regina Hall
Editorial Director: Lee E. Hassig

WILLIAMS-SONOMA

Founder/Vice-Chairman: Chuck Williams

WELDON OWEN INC.

President: John Owen
Publisher: Wendely Harvey
Senior Editor: Laurie Wertz
Consulting Editor: Norman Kolpas
Copy Editor: Sharon Silva
Recipe Translation: Barbara McGilvray
Design: John Bull, The Book Design Company
Production: Stephanie Sherman, Mick Bagnato
Food Photographer: Allan Rosenberg
Associate Food Photographer: Allen V. Lott
Primary Food & Prop Stylist: Sandra Griswold
Food Stylist: Heidi Gintner
Prop Assistant: Karen Nicks
Glossary Illustrations: Alice Harth

The Williams-Sonoma Kitchen Library
conceived and produced by Weldon Owen Inc.
814 Montgomery St., San Francisco, CA 94133

In collaboration with Williams-Sonoma
100 North Point, San Francisco, CA 94133

Production by Mandarin Offset, Hong Kong
Printed in Hong Kong

A Weldon Owen Production

Copyright © 1992 Weldon Owen Inc.
Reprinted in 1992

Library of Congress
Cataloging-in-Publication Data:

Hors d'oeuvres & appetizers / general editor,
  Chuck Williams ; recipes, the Scotto Sisters ;
  photographs, Allan Rosenberg.
       p.   cm. — (Williams-Sonoma kitchen
    library)
    Includes index.
    ISBN 0-7835-0218-4
  —ISBN 0-7835-0219-2 (pbk.)
    1. Appetizers. I. Williams, Chuck.
II. Scotto Sisters. III. Title: Hors d'oeuvres
and appetizers. IV. Series.
TX740.H619   1992
641.8'12—dc20   92-8505
                                 CIP

Contents

CHEESES & EGGS 15

VEGETABLES 37

FISH & SHELLFISH 57

POULTRY & MEAT 81

INTRODUCTION

Many of us enjoy serving and eating hors d'oeuvres and appetizers, yet few of us are aware that the French term *hors-d'oeuvre* literally means "outside the work"—dishes usually served and eaten apart from the main meal.

That translation, I think, sums up the widespread appeal that hors d'oeuvres and appetizers enjoy; they are, quite simply, liberating. You can prepare and serve them with ease as the featured attraction of a cocktail party or informal buffet—the classic role of hors d'oeuvres. Or you can present them as the first course of a meal—that is, as appetizers. But hors d'oeuvres and appetizers needn't be confined to those roles; indeed you can make up an entire meal based on them alone.

To help you plan a varied party selection, choose the perfect first course, or compose a light, well-balanced meal, the 45 main recipes in this book are conveniently organized by featured ingredient—cheeses and eggs; vegetables; fish and shellfish; poultry and meat. There's also a comprehensive guide to the equipment you'll need to prepare and serve them, along with guidelines for making the basic pastries, breads and blini that are integral parts of so many recipes.

Every one of the dishes in this book has been created not only to be delicious, but also to be exceptionally easy to prepare. With that in mind, let me offer one final word of encouragement: Try a selection of these recipes as soon as possible, perhaps even for dinner tonight.

I'm sure you'll agree that well-chosen hors d'oeuvres and appetizers are capable of making any party or meal feel like a special occasion.

Chuck Williams

EQUIPMENT

Everything you need to prepare all kinds of hors d'oeuvres and appetizers, from cutting and mixing to final presentation

The array of equipment shown here makes all the work of mixing, cooking, garnishing and presenting hors d'oeuvres and appetizers as easy as possible.

Of course, most such recipes are fairly simple—there's little point in making hors d'oeuvres or appetizers so labor-intensive that they prevent your enjoyment of the meal or party. Most of the equipment is used for basic cutting and mixing—knives, bowls, spatulas, whisks and so on.

Many of the tools shown here devote themselves to presentation—from glazing brushes to piping bags, serving dishes to paper doilies. After all, hors d'oeuvres and appetizers are meant to whet the appetite, and visual flair is an important part of their appeal.

1. Rubber Spatulas
For blending sauces or purées, scraping out bowls, transferring mixtures and smoothing finished dishes. Available in varied sizes; large scoop is good for heavy batters or doughs. Choose sturdy, pliable rubber or silicone heads.

2. Dowel-Type Rolling Pin
For best control when rolling out doughs. Select a sturdy hardwood pin, at least 12 inches (30 cm) long. To prevent warping, do not wash; wipe clean with a dry cloth.

3. Food Processor
Quickly chops, purées, shreds, grates or blends large quantities of ingredients.

4. Bowl or Board Scraper
Sturdy, curved plastic blade scrapes bowls or work surfaces.

5. Garlic Press
Mashes fresh garlic cloves. Choose one—usually cast aluminum—that feels comfortable in the hand and has a sturdy, durable hinge and a plastic cleaning tool.

6. Piping Bags and Tips
Plastic-lined cloth or all-plastic bags and stainless-steel tips enable easy, accurate piping of chou pastry or fillings. Choose larger bags, which are easier to fill and handle.

7. Feather Pastry Brush
Delicate brush smoothly applies gelatin glazes, free of brush marks.

8. All-Purpose Pastry Brushes
For general basting and glazing. Choose sturdy brushes with well-attached natural bristles.

9. Decorative Cutting Tools
Small tools with sharp stainless-steel edges and sturdy handles cut (left to right) balls, citrus zests, strips of citrus peel.

10. Miniature Muffin Pan
Bakes tartlets and miniature quiches and pizzas. Nonstick aluminum conducts heat well. Also available in plain tinplate and aluminum.

11. Baking Sheet
Nonstick aluminum, for quick baking of small hors d'oeuvres.

15. Icing Spatula
Long blade smooths glazes or purées and doubles as a spatula.

16. Hors d'Oeuvre Dishes
Rectangular glass or porcelain dishes, also known by the French *raviers* or as Italian antipasti dishes, are attractive for serving an array of hors d'oeuvres in a limited space.

17. Pouring Bowls
Sturdy plastic in 3 sizes for mixing small amounts of sauces and fillings. Lips enable easy pouring.

18. Electric Deep Fryer
Covered model eliminates splattering and odors; temperature control and timer produce reliable results.

19. Terrine
Traditional French earthenware container for terrines and pâtés. Comes in varied shapes and sizes, and in porcelain or glass.

20. Mixing Bowl
Large bowl for mixing ingredients in quantity. Traditional earthenware design includes angled base that allows tilting for easier mixing or beating.

21. All-Purpose Knives
For general preparation. Choose good-quality stain-resistant steel blades with firmly anchored, comfortable handles.

22. Paper Doilies
For decorative presentations—especially fried foods, whose surface oil they absorb.

12. Wire Cooling Rack
Allows air to circulate around delicate pastries as they cool, preserving crispness. For small hors d'oeuvres, choose one with a small, square-patterned wire mesh rather than a parallel wire grid. Keep several on hand to accommodate large batches.

13. Wire Whisks
Larger balloon whisk incorporates air into beaten egg whites. Smaller whisk stirs sauces for extra smoothness.

14. Serrated Knives
Sharp serrations easily cut bread, tomatoes or cucumbers into thin, even slices.

Tart Pastry

PÂTE BRISÉE

Tender, flaky and buttery, this classic dough forms the foundation for all manner of miniature quiches and other little tartlets (see recipes on pages 19 and 34). The dough should be made at least 3 hours ahead, or preferably the night before, so it has time to chill. It may be stored in a plastic bag for up to 4 days in the refrigerator or for up to 2 months in the freezer.

1½ cups (6 oz/180 g) all-purpose (plain) flour
2 pinches of salt
6 tablespoons (3 oz/100 g) unsalted butter, at room
   temperature, cut into rough chunks
1 small egg

To make the dough in a food processor, put the flour and salt into the work bowl fitted with a metal blade and pulse a few times to mix. Add the butter and egg and pulse briefly just until the mixture comes together in a ball.

To make the dough by hand, place the flour, salt and butter in a large bowl. With your fingertips mix the ingredients together until the butter is broken into large flakes coated with flour. Add the egg and continue to mix until the ingredients are the consistency of coarse crumbs. Gather the dough into a ball.

Put the ball of dough into a plastic bag and let it rest in the refrigerator for at least 3 hours before using. Remove the dough from the refrigerator about 30 minutes before rolling it out.

Makes 11 oz (350 g) dough

1. *Combining the ingredients.* Put flour and salt in the bowl of a processor fitted with a metal blade; pulse a few times to combine. Add the chunks of butter and break in the egg.

2. *Mixing the dough.* Pulse the machine until the ingredients resemble coarse, moist crumbs, stopping several times to scrape the bowl as necessary. Process continuously just until dough forms a ball that rides around the bowl on the blade.

3. *Rolling out the dough.* Roll out on a lightly floured work surface, working from the center outward and giving the dough a quarter turn after each roll, until thickness specified in individual recipes.

Cheese Puffs

Blue Cheese Tartlets

8

Puff Shell Pastry

PÂTE À CHOUX

With its high proportion of eggs, butter and water, which are heated together with the flour during the preparation of the dough, the classic French chou pastry puffs up into light, airy, well-rounded shapes (chou is French for "cabbage"). The pastry is the basis for the classic light hors d'oeuvre of cheese puffs (recipe on page 26). The dough may be stored in a plastic bag for 2 days in the refrigerator or for up to 2 months in the freezer.

6 tablespoons (3 oz/100 g) unsalted butter, cut into
    small dice
1 cup (8 fl oz/250 ml) water
1 teaspoon salt
1¼ cups (5 oz/150 g) all-purpose (plain) flour
5 eggs

*I*n a saucepan combine the butter, water and salt. Bring to a boil over medium heat, stirring often, and remove from the heat. Immediately pour in the flour all at once and stir vigorously with a wooden spoon until you have a smooth mixture. Put the pan back on gentle heat and continue to stir until there are no lumps and the mixture pulls away from the pan sides, 1 minute.

Remove from the heat and add the eggs, one at a time, making sure each egg is thoroughly mixed in before adding the next. Work the dough as little as possible after adding the first egg. The dough should be shiny and be stiff enough to hold a shape.

The dough is now ready to be used. It can be formed by spoonfuls or with a pastry bag fitted with a plain or decorative tip. The dough should be spooned or piped onto parchment-lined baking sheets or nonstick baking sheets.

Makes 1 lb (500 g) dough

1. *Combining the ingredients.*
Put the butter, water and salt into a heavy saucepan. Bring to a boil over medium heat, stirring frequently to help the butter melt evenly. Remove from the heat and immediately add flour.

2. *Adding the eggs.*
Break an egg into a small bowl. Add the egg to the pan, beating vigorously just until smoothly incorporated. In the same way, add remaining eggs, one at a time.

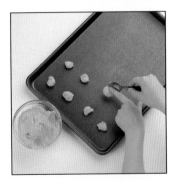

3. *Spooning the dough.*
To shape with a spoon, push individual spoonfuls with your fingertip onto a nonstick or parchment paper-lined baking sheet; bake according to recipe instructions.

4. *Piping the dough.*
Alternatively, shape the paste with a pastry bag: Fit bag with plain or decorative no. 6 tip and twist tip and bag to close while filling. Fold back top and spoon in paste to fill halfway; then hold top of bag by its edges and shake over a bowl or sink to remove air pockets. Twist bag shut, untwist tip, and squeeze gently but firmly to pipe.

Pizza Dough
PÂTE À PIZZA

Pizza is undeniably one of the world's favorite foods. Prepared in miniature, with a variety of toppings, it makes an outstanding hors d'oeuvre (see recipes on pages 38, 51 and 96). The base is a simple yeast-leavened dough, which takes some time to rise but is fairly easy to mix by hand, as shown here. The dough may be stored in a plastic bag for up to 2 days in the refrigerator or for up to 2 months in the freezer. The recipes that call for this dough use slightly less than the 1 lb (450 g) yield. Use the leftover dough to make an extra, larger pizza or store it as described above. Let it defrost overnight in the refrigerator before use.

½ teaspoon sugar
¾ cup (6 fl oz/175 ml) warm water (95°F/35°C)
1 package (scant 1 tablespoon/¼ oz/8 g) active dry
   yeast
2⅓ cups (10 oz/300 g) all-purpose (plain) flour
1 teaspoon fine sea salt

1. Proofing the yeast.
In a small glass or bowl, dissolve sugar in warm water. Sprinkle yeast over the water and leave undisturbed at warm room temperature until yeast foams.

2. Kneading the dough.
Push dough forward from its center with the heel of your hand, then fold it back over, give it a quarter turn, and repeat until smooth and elastic.

Put the sugar in a glass that holds about ¾ cup (7 fl oz/200 ml). Add a scant ½ cup (3½ fl oz/100 ml) of the warm water and stir with a small spoon to dissolve the sugar. Sprinkle the yeast over the surface and let stand in a warm place, without touching it, for 10 minutes. It should foam up to reach the rim of the glass.

Now heap the flour on a work surface. Scatter the salt over it and then mix it into the flour. Make a well in the center. With a small spoon stir the yeast mixture in the glass and then pour it into the well together with the remaining warm water. Mix these ingredients together with your fingertips, using a rapid circular movement and working from the center of the well outward. When well mixed, roll the dough into a ball and, on a lightly floured surface, knead it as follows: with the heel of your hand, push it far away from you, then fold it over,

at the same time giving it a counterclockwise quarter turn. Continue to work the dough in this manner until it is smooth and elastic, 5–6 minutes. If the dough is too sticky, add a little flour until smooth. If too dry, add a few drops of water. Place the dough in a large, lightly floured bowl and cover the bowl with a cloth. Let it rest in a warm place, protected from drafts, until doubled in bulk, about 1½ hours. Tap the dough with your fingertips to deflate it, and then transfer it to a lightly floured work surface. Knead as before for 3 minutes. The dough is now ready to be rolled out.

Makes 1 lb (450 g) dough

3. Leaving the dough to rise.
Gather together kneaded dough into a ball and transfer to a large, lightly floured bowl. Cover with a kitchen towel and place away from drafts at warm room temperature.

4. Punching down the dough.
With your fingertips tap the risen dough down in its center to deflate it.

5. Cutting out the dough.
For miniature pizzas roll out dough on a lightly floured surface. With a floured round pastry cutter, cut out rounds.

Onion Tartlet

Mini Pizzas with Mozzarella

11

Yogurt Quick Bread

PAIN RAPIDE AU YAOURT

So simple and quick, this recipe allows you to serve fresh-baked, flavorful bread with virtually any spread or other dish that calls for plain or toasted slices. The dough can be formed into any shape desired and baked on a baking sheet, or it can be put into a bread tin or muffin pan.

1 cup (8 oz/250 g) plain yogurt, at room temperature
1⅔ cups (7 oz/200 g) all-purpose (plain) flour
1⅔ cups (7 oz/200 g) whole-wheat flour
4 teaspoons baking soda
1 teaspoon salt
2 teaspoons superfine (caster) sugar
¼ cup (2 fl oz/60 ml) peanut oil or vegetable oil
1 egg
1 tablespoon water

Preheat an oven to 450°F (225°C).

In a small bowl beat the yogurt with a fork until it is smooth. Sift together the flours, baking soda, salt and sugar onto a work surface. Make a well in the center and add the yogurt and oil to it. Mix these ingredients together with your fingertips, using a rapid circular movement and working from the center of the well outward. When well mixed, knead the dough on a lightly floured surface, stretching it out in front of you and then rolling it into a ball, until it becomes very smooth and pulls away from your fingers, 7–8 minutes.

Shape the dough as desired and place on a nonstick baking sheet or in a bread pan or muffin pans. In a small bowl beat together the egg and water with a fork. Brush the egg mixture over the surface of the dough. Bake until browned, 25–35 minutes, depending upon the size of the loaf. Invert onto a wire rack to cool.

Makes 1 large loaf or 6 rolls

Blini

The small, quickly prepared pancakes generally known by the Russian name blini provide attractive bases for hors d'oeuvres—particularly those featuring seafood, such as taramasalata (page 60), potted smoked trout (page 78) and smoked salmon mousse (page 57). The same batter can be used to make crêpes, in which case you will need to use an 8-inch (20-cm) crêpe pan. Heat the pan with butter and add enough batter to coat the bottom, tilting it to form a very thin, even sheet. The cooking time is about the same as for blini, but you will have to add more butter to the pan as needed to prevent the crêpes from sticking. The batter keeps well for a day or so, refrigerated in a covered bowl.

Yogurt Quick Bread

1. Mixing the batter.
Put flour, milk, eggs and butter in the work bowl of a food processor fitted with a metal blade. Process until well mixed.

2. Forming the blini.
With a small ladle, pour batter into pan to form rounds, making as many as will fit comfortably in the pan without touching.

3. Turning the blini.
Cook the blini until covered with bubbles and edges look dry. With a long spatula, flip them over.

4. Finishing and storing blini.
Cook the blini until undersides are golden brown. Serve immediately, or let the blini cool and then stack between squares of waxed paper. Freeze in airtight plastic bags. To use, remove bags and paper and gently warm in the oven.

¾ cup (3 oz/100 g) all-purpose (plain) flour
1 cup (8 fl oz/250 ml) milk
2 eggs
¼ cup (2 oz/50 g) unsalted butter, melted and cooled,
  plus 2–3 tablespoons for cooking the blini

Combine the flour, milk, eggs and the ¼ cup melted butter in the work bowl of a food processor fitted with a metal blade, or in a blender. Process until well mixed. Pass the batter through a fine-mesh strainer into a bowl to remove any lumps.

To cook the blini, melt the 2 tablespoons butter in a large nonstick frying pan over medium heat. With a small ladle, drop spoonfuls of the batter onto the pan, forming rounds about 2 inches (5 cm) in diameter, or up to 4 inches (10 cm) in diameter, if you wish. When bubbles form on the top and the edges look dry, after about 1 minute, use a spatula to turn the blini over. Continue cooking until the undersides are golden brown, about 1 minute more. Remove the blini to a platter. Cook the remaining batter, adding butter to the pan as needed. Serve immediately.

Makes 48 2-inch (5-cm) blini or 12 8-inch (20-cm) crêpes; serves 6–8

*Smoked Salmon
Mousse*

13

Crisp Ricotta Rolls with Walnuts and Chives

PETITS ROULEAUX AU FROMAGE, NOIX ET HERBES

¾ cup (7 oz/200 g) ricotta
⅓ cup (1 oz/25 g) walnut halves
2 oz (50 g) Emmenthaler cheese
freshly grated zest of 1 lemon
2 pinches of freshly grated nutmeg
4 pinches of ground cinnamon
2 tablespoons snipped fresh chives
salt and freshly ground pepper
6 sheets filo pastry
1 tablespoon peanut oil or vegetable oil

Delicate filo dough forms the crisp wrapper for a creamy ricotta mixture.

*P*reheat an oven to 425°F (225°C). In a bowl mash the ricotta with a fork. Using a rotary grater fitted with the large-holed disk, grate first the walnuts and then the Emmenthaler into the bowl containing the ricotta. Alternatively, grate them in a food processor fitted with a shredding disk. Add the lemon zest, nutmeg, cinnamon, chives and salt and pepper to taste. Mix well.

Cut the filo sheets in half crosswise. Place a half sheet on a work surface, keeping the remaining sheets covered with a damp towel so they do not dry out. On half of the sheet, spread one-twelfth of the cheese mixture in a rectangle about 3 inches (7.5 cm) long and ¾ inch (2 cm) wide, leaving the bottom edge and sides uncovered. Fold the bottom edge over the mixture, then fold in the sides and roll up into a cylinder about 1½ inches (4 cm) in diameter. Repeat with the remaining sheets and cheese mixture.

Using a pastry brush, oil a baking sheet with some of the oil. Arrange the rolls on the baking sheet at least ½ inch (12 mm) apart. Lightly brush the pastries with the remaining oil. Transfer the baking sheet to the oven and bake until golden and crisp, 18–20 minutes. Serve while still crisp, either hot or warm.

Makes 12 rolls; serves 6

Mozzarella and Tomato Crostini

CROSTINI À LA MOZZARELLA

2 tablespoons unsalted butter

6 slices white sandwich bread

3 perfectly ripe plum (egg) tomatoes, thinly sliced crosswise

1 tablespoon extra-virgin olive oil

dried oregano

salt and freshly ground pepper

10 oz (300 g) mozzarella

12 anchovy fillets in olive oil, drained

For this simple and popular Italian antipasto, bread slices are topped with mozzarella cheese and sun-ripened tomato and baked until crisp. Assemble them up to 1 hour in advance, if you like, to be put into the oven when guests arrive. They are also delicious with other good-melting cheeses such as jack, Swiss or mild Cheddar. The anchovies are optional. Serve the crostini hot from the oven or warm.

Preheat an oven to 350°F (175°C). Butter the bread slices on one side and cut in half. Lay the bread pieces on a baking sheet, buttered side up. Place the tomato slices in a shallow dish and sprinkle them with the olive oil. Sprinkle with oregano, salt and pepper to taste and toss gently.

Cut the mozzarella into 12 thin slices to fit the bread pieces and top each piece of bread with a slice of mozzarella.

Place an anchovy fillet on top of each cheese slice. Arrange 1 or 2 tomato slices on top. Transfer the baking sheet to the oven and bake until the bread is thoroughly heated and the mozzarella is almost melted, about 5 minutes.

Makes 12 crostini; serves 6

Blue Cheese Tartlets

TARTELETTES AU BLEU

8 oz (250 g) tart pastry dough *(recipe on page 8)* or commercial puff pastry

3 oz (100 g) spinach or Swiss chard (silverbeet), trimmed

1 egg

⅔ cup (5 fl oz/150 ml) heavy (double) cream

¾ cup (3 oz/100 g) freshly grated Emmenthaler cheese

¼ teaspoon freshly grated nutmeg

salt and freshly ground pepper

3 oz (100 g) Roquefort cheese, crumbled

2 tablespoons pine nuts

The robust flavor of spinach or Swiss chard is more than a match for the tang of blue cheese in these bite-sized tarts.

*I*f using tart pastry, prepare the dough and refrigerate for at least 3 hours. Remove from the refrigerator 30 minutes before you are ready to roll it out. If using commercial puff pastry, defrost in the refrigerator or at room temperature.

Preheat an oven to 425°F (225°C). Bring a large saucepan filled with water to a boil. Plunge the spinach or Swiss chard into the boiling water and cook for 30 seconds. Immediately drain in a colander and rinse with cold water to halt the cooking. Drain again, pressing against the greens to force out as much water as possible; set aside.

Break the egg into a bowl. Add the cream, Emmenthaler cheese, nutmeg and salt and pepper to taste and beat with a fork until completely blended. Coarsely chop the spinach or chard and add it to the bowl; stir well.

On a lightly floured board, roll the dough out as thinly as possible. Sprinkle the Roquefort evenly over the dough. With a fluted pastry cutter about 1¼ inches (4 cm) in diameter, cut out 18 dough rounds. Use the rounds to line 18 individual tartlet pans or the wells in tartlet trays or miniature muffin pans. If using the former, arrange the lined pans on a large baking sheet. Fill each lined pan with some of the egg mixture and scatter a few pine nuts on top. Place the tartlets in the oven and bake until the filling sets and the crust is golden, about 15 minutes. Serve warm.

Makes 18 tartlets; serves 6

Crab Omelet with Sweet-and-Sour Sauce

OMELETTE AU CRABE, SAUCE AIGRE-DOUCE

3 tablespoons extra-virgin olive oil, plus
    extra for plate
1 lb (500 g) red sweet peppers
    (capsicums), stemmed, seeded,
    deribbed and cut into ⅜-inch (1-cm)
    squares
3 tablespoons water
½ teaspoon superfine (caster) sugar
salt
9 eggs
freshly ground pepper
1 clove garlic, cut into tiny matchsticks
13 oz (400 g) cooked crab meat, flaked
1 teaspoon sweet paprika
4 pinches of hot paprika
3 tablespoons tomato sauce (puréed
    tomatoes)

FOR THE SAUCE:
½ cup (4 fl oz/100 ml) rice vinegar
2 tablespoons superfine (caster) sugar
¾ cup (7 fl oz/200 ml) tomato sauce
    (puréed tomatoes)

*P*our 2 tablespoons of the olive oil into a medium nonstick frying pan. Add the sweet peppers, water, sugar and salt to taste. Bring to a boil, stir well, cover with a lid slightly ajar and cook over medium heat, turning often, until the peppers begin to brown, about 10 minutes.

Meanwhile, break the eggs into a large bowl. Add salt and pepper to taste and the remaining 1 tablespoon olive oil and beat with a fork until completely blended. Set aside.

Add the garlic to the frying pan and stir for 1 minute. Add the crab meat and cook and stir for 3 minutes; add the sweet and hot paprikas and mix again. Now stir in the tomato sauce, followed by the beaten eggs. When the eggs begin to set, smooth the surface with the back of a spoon and cover the pan. Cook over low heat for 8 minutes.

Lightly oil a plate. When the omelet is ready, invert it onto the plate. Slide it back into the pan, browned side up, and cook, covered, over low heat for another 8 minutes. Transfer to the plate and let cool to room temperature.

To make the sauce, combine the vinegar and sugar in a small, heavy saucepan and bring to a boil over low heat. Cook until the mixture is syrupy, 2–3 minutes. Add the tomato sauce and boil for 1 minute longer, then remove the pan from the heat and cool to room temperature.

Just before serving, cut the omelet into cubes and spoon the sauce into a small serving bowl. Spear the omelet cubes with toothpicks and dip into the sauce.

Serves 8

Potato Omelet

OMELETTE AUX POMMES DE TERRE RAPÉES

1 lb (500 g) baking potatoes, peeled
½ cup (4 fl oz/100 ml) water
1 tablespoon unsalted butter
3 tablespoons extra-virgin olive oil, plus
  extra for plate
salt
1 clove garlic
2 tablespoons snipped fresh parsley
6 eggs
freshly ground pepper
¼ teaspoon freshly grated nutmeg

Flat vegetable omelets such as this one are eaten throughout southwestern Europe. The omelet may also be cut into wedges and served as a first course.

In a food processor fitted with the appropriate disk or with a sharp knife, cut the potatoes into matchstick lengths.

Pour the water into a small nonstick frying pan and add the butter and 2 tablespoons of the oil. Bring to a boil and add the potatoes. Stir well and sprinkle with salt. Cover with a lid slightly ajar and cook over medium heat, turning often, until just crisp and the water evaporates, about 12 minutes. Add the garlic by passing it through a garlic press. Add the parsley. Continue to cook and stir for 3 minutes.

Meanwhile, break the eggs into a large bowl. Add salt and pepper to taste, the nutmeg and the remaining 1 tablespoon oil and beat with a fork until the eggs are completely blended. Pour the eggs over the potatoes and, when they begin to set, smooth the surface with the back of a spoon and cover the pan. Cook over low heat for 8 minutes.

Lightly oil a plate large enough to hold the omelet. When the omelet is ready, invert it onto the oiled plate. Slide it back into the pan, browned side up, and cook, covered, over low heat for another 8 minutes. Transfer the omelet to the plate and cut into cubes or small triangles. Serve warm or at room temperature with toothpicks.

Serves 6

Blue Cheese Spread with Walnuts

CRÈME DE FROMAGES

12 walnut halves

1 lb (500 g) soft white cheese such as cream cheese or ricotta, at room temperature

5 oz (150 g) blue cheese such as Roquefort or Gorgonzola, at room temperature

1 tablespoon Cognac or Armagnac

salt and freshly ground pepper

1 bunch fresh chives, finely chopped

Walnuts and blue cheese—whether Roquefort, Gorgonzola, Stilton or another variety—are a favorite European pairing. Serve with yogurt quick bread (recipe on page 12), toasted whole-grain country bread, breadsticks or fresh vegetables.

With a rotary grater fitted with the large-holed disk or in the work bowl of a food processor fitted with a shredding disk, grate the walnuts; set aside.

Combine the white and blue cheeses in a dish and mash them together with a fork, incorporating the Cognac or Armagnac and a little salt and pepper. When the mixture is smooth, add the walnuts and chives. Mix again until well blended. Spoon into a serving bowl.

Serves 8

Cheese Puffs

PETITS CHOUX AU FROMAGE

1 lb (500 g) puff shell pastry (recipe on
   page 9)
1 cup (4 oz/125 g) freshly grated
   Emmenthaler or Gruyère cheese
¼ teaspoon freshly grated nutmeg
freshly ground white pepper

*Egg-laced pastry dough, mixed with grated Emmenthaler or
Gruyère cheese and piped onto a cookie sheet, puffs up in the
oven to form light, flaky, flavorful spheres—classic French
hors d'oeuvres that are good hot or at room temperature.
Any fairly firm, flavorful cheese that can be grated, such as
Cheddar or Comté, can be substituted.*

*P*repare the pastry dough. While it is still hot, vigorously
beat in the cheese, nutmeg and pepper to taste with a
rubber spatula.

   Preheat an oven to 450°F (230°C). Spoon the dough into
a pastry bag fitted with a plain tip ⅝ inch (1.5 cm) in
diameter. Pipe small rounds about 1½ inches (4 cm) in
diameter onto a nonstick baking sheet at about 2-inch
(5-cm) intervals. Alternatively, pipe the mixture into
muffin-tin wells.

   Transfer the baking sheet to the oven and bake until the
pastry is puffed and golden, 15–20 minutes. If serving at
room temperature, cool on wire racks.

Makes about 30 puffs; serves 6

Terrine of Mediterranean Mixed Vegetables

RATATOUILLE EN TERRINE

3 tablespoons extra-virgin olive oil, plus
  extra for baking dish
8 oz (250 g) small white onions, about
  ¾ inch (2 cm) in diameter, thinly
  sliced
1¼ lb (600 g) plump red and green
  sweet peppers (capsicums), stemmed,
  seeded, deribbed and cut into
  ⅜-inch (1-cm) squares
11 oz (350 g) eggplants (aubergines),
  trimmed and cut into ⅜-inch (1-cm)
  dice
13 oz (400 g) zucchini (courgettes),
  trimmed and cut into ⅜-inch (1-cm)
  dice
8 oz (250 g) plum (egg) tomatoes,
  peeled, seeded and cut into ⅜-inch
  (1-cm) dice
1 teaspoon fresh thyme leaves or
  ¼ teaspoon dried thyme
salt and freshly ground pepper
6 eggs
1 clove garlic, finely chopped
2 tablespoons chopped fresh basil

Think of this baked flat omelet as an elegant variation on the classic Provençal ratatouille.

*H*eat the 3 tablespoons olive oil in a medium nonstick frying pan over medium heat. Add the onions and cook, stirring, until they begin to color, about 3 minutes. Add the sweet peppers and stir for 5 minutes. Add the eggplants and again stir for 5 minutes. Add the zucchini, tomatoes, thyme and salt and pepper to taste. Stir well, cover and cook for 30 minutes, stirring from time to time.

Meanwhile, break the eggs into a bowl. Season them with salt and pepper to taste and beat with a fork until blended.

Preheat an oven to 350°F (175°C). Oil an 8-by-12-inch (20-by-30-cm) baking dish.

When the vegetables have been cooking for 30 minutes, stir in the garlic and basil and then the eggs. Mix thoroughly and remove the pan from the heat. Pour the mixture into the prepared baking dish and cover with a sheet of aluminum foil pricked all over with the tip of a knife.

Transfer the baking dish to the oven and bake until set, about 45 minutes. Remove from the oven and allow to cool completely in the dish. Refrigerate for 6 hours before serving. To serve, turn the terrine out onto a plate and cut it into slices. Cut the slices into cubes and serve with toothpicks.

Serves 8

Two-Cheese Balls
BOUCHÉES AUX DEUX FROMAGES

2 egg whites
¾ cup (3 oz/100 g) freshly grated
   Emmenthaler cheese
½ cup (2 oz/50 g) freshly grated
   Parmesan cheese
salt and freshly ground pepper
¼ teaspoon freshly grated nutmeg
peanut oil or vegetable oil for
   deep-frying

Mild, slightly nutty-tasting Emmenthaler combines with tangy Parmesan in these creamy, deep-fried bites of cheese. You can use Swiss or Gruyère in place of the Emmenthaler.

*P*ut the egg whites into a large bowl and beat with a fork until they begin to froth. Add the cheeses, salt and pepper to taste, and nutmeg. Work these ingredients together with your hands until they form a soft, well-blended mixture.

   Scoop up a teaspoonful of the cheese mixture and roll it between your palms into a ball. Continue to shape the rest of the mixture in the same manner; you will have about 20 small balls in all.

   Pour the oil into a deep-fat fryer or a heavy saucepan to a depth of at least 2 inches (5 cm). Place the pan over medium heat until the oil reaches 350°F (180°C), or until a small bit of bread tossed into the oil surfaces immediately. When the oil is ready, carefully slip the cheese balls, 5 or 6 at a time, into the hot oil and cook, turning them with a slotted spoon, until they are golden, 4 or 5 minutes.

   With a slotted spoon remove the cheese balls to paper towels to drain. Repeat with the remaining balls. Arrange on a serving plate and serve warm or at room temperature.

Makes 20 balls; serves 6

Eggs Mimosa with Tuna Filling
OEUFS MIMOSA À LA CRÈME DE THON

8 eggs, hard-cooked

5 oz (150 g) canned tuna in water, well drained

2 tablespoons cream cheese, at room temperature

2 tablespoons extra-virgin olive oil

1 tablespoon dark rum (optional)

1 teaspoon curry powder

salt and freshly ground pepper

1 lemon or lime

1 tablespoon tiny capers in brine, rinsed and well drained

The name for this traditional stuffed-egg preparation derives from the mimosa tree's frothy yellow flowers, which the egg yolks—pressed through a strainer—closely resemble. If you like, add a few drained anchovy fillets to the filling mixture.

Shell the eggs and cut them in half lengthwise. Remove the yolks and reserve 3 of them for the mimosa; put the rest into the work bowl of a food processor fitted with a metal blade or into a blender. Set the egg whites aside.

Add the tuna, cheese, olive oil, rum, curry powder and salt and pepper to taste to the food processor. Grate the zest of the lemon into the processor bowl, then halve the lemon and squeeze it to extract 1 tablespoon juice. Add the juice to the processor bowl along with the capers. Process at medium speed until you have a thick cream, about 1 minute. The mixture must not be too liquid.

Fill the egg-white halves with the tuna mixture, using enough of the mixture to round the top so that it looks like the original egg shape. Arrange the stuffed eggs on a large, flat plate. Put the reserved yolks in a stainless-steel fine-mesh strainer held over the stuffed eggs and crush the yolks with the back of a spoon, forcing them through the mesh so that the stuffed eggs are evenly covered with the sieved yolks, or mimosa. Keep in a cool place until ready to serve.

Serves 8

Mini Quiches Lorraines

8 oz (250 g) tart pastry dough (*recipe on page 8*)

7 oz (225 g) lean smoked bacon, very thinly sliced and cut into ¼-inch (6-mm) pieces

3 eggs

4 pinches freshly grated nutmeg

salt and freshly ground pepper

¾ cup (7 fl oz/200 ml) heavy (double) cream

The classic French quiche filling used in these bite-sized pastries may be dressed up with the addition of a little shredded Gruyère cheese. You can make the quiches in advance and reheat them in a preheated 425°F (225°C) oven just as the guests arrive.

Prepare the pastry dough and refrigerate for at least 3 hours. Remove the pastry dough from the refrigerator at least 30 minutes before you are ready to roll it out.

Preheat an oven to 425°F (225°C). On a lightly floured board roll out the dough as thinly as possible. With a fluted pastry cutter about 1¼ inches (4 cm) in diameter, cut out 18 rounds. Use the rounds to line 18 individual tartlet pans or the wells in tartlet trays or miniature muffin pans. If using the former, arrange the pans on a large baking sheet.

In a small nonstick frying pan over medium heat, fry the bacon, stirring often, until crisp, about 5 minutes. With a slotted spoon, remove the crisp bacon pieces to paper towels to drain.

Break the eggs into a bowl. Add the nutmeg and salt and pepper to taste and beat with a fork until completely blended. Continuing to beat, add the cream in a thin, steady stream.

Distribute the bacon pieces evenly among the pastry-lined pans, then pour in the cream mixture. Place the quiches in the oven and bake until the filling sets and the crusts are golden, about 15 minutes. Serve hot or warm.

Makes 18 mini quiches; serves 6

Stuffed Cherry Tomatoes
TOMATES CERISE FARCIES

36 cherry tomatoes, about 1½ oz
  (40 g) each

FOR THE OLIVE STUFFING:
6 boned and skinned canned sardines in
  olive oil, well drained and tails
  discarded
3 tablespoons (2 oz/50 g) black olive
  paste
1 tablespoon chopped celery leaves
3 gherkins, finely chopped
¼ teaspoon cayenne pepper

FOR THE CHEESE STUFFING:
13 oz (400 g) fresh goat's milk cheese,
  such as Brousse de brebis, or ricotta,
  drained
2 tablespoons extra-virgin olive oil
2 green (spring) onions, finely chopped,
  including the green portions
1 tablespoon snipped fresh summer
  savory or parsley
freshly ground pepper

Two different stuffings—one based on black olives, the other on creamy goat's milk cheese—add variety in flavor and color. For an even more stunning presentation, look for the miniature yellow tomatoes that are becoming more widely available. The fillings are also excellent scooped into or served as dips for other vegetables, such as celery sticks or wedges of sweet pepper (capsicum).

Cut a small cap from the top of each tomato. With a small spoon scoop out the flesh (reserve for another use). Invert the hollowed-out tomatoes on a plate to drain.

To make the olive stuffing, place the sardines in a bowl and mash them with a fork. Add the olive paste, celery leaves, gherkins and cayenne pepper and mix well. Fill 18 of the tomatoes with this stuffing.

To make the cheese stuffing, place the cheese in a bowl and mash it with a fork. Add the olive oil, green onions, summer savory and pepper. Mix well. Fill the remaining 18 tomatoes with this stuffing.

Serve the tomatoes cold.

Makes 36 stuffed tomatoes; serves 6–8

Mini Pizzas with Mozzarella

MINI PIZZAS À LA MOZZARELLA

13 oz (400 g) pizza dough (recipe on
page 10)

1¼ lb (600 g) ripe but firm tomatoes,
cut in half crosswise, seeded and cut
into thin strips

6 oz (200 g) mozzarella cheese, cut
into thin strips

12 anchovy fillets in olive oil, drained
and finely diced

2 tablespoons extra-virgin olive oil

1 teaspoon dried oregano

freshly ground pepper

24 black olives, pitted

*Topped with tomato, mozzarella, anchovies, black olives,
oregano and a drizzle of olive oil, these mini pies represent
pizza in its most basic—and memorable—Neapolitan form.
Leave out the anchovies if you wish, or add some shavings
of Parmesan cheese. If necessary, the pizzas can be reheated
at the last moment in a preheated 425°F (225°C) oven for
6–8 minutes.*

*P*repare the pizza dough. Preheat an oven to 500°F
(250°C).

On a lightly floured work surface, roll out the dough
⅜ inch (1 cm) thick. With a round pastry cutter 1½ inches
(4 cm) in diameter, cut out 24 rounds. Now roll these
rounds out again until they are 3⁄16 inch (.5 cm) thick. Lay
the rounds on a nonstick baking sheet.

Place the tomatoes in a bowl. Add the mozzarella and
anchovies and toss lightly. Drizzle with the olive oil and
sprinkle with the oregano and pepper to taste; mix gently.

Divide the tomato mixture evenly among the dough
rounds and top each with an olive. Transfer the baking
sheet to the oven and bake the pizzas until the cheese melts
and the edges of the crust are golden, about 15 minutes.
Serve warm.

Makes 24 mini pizzas; serves 8

Guacamole

2 perfectly ripe avocados, 8 oz (250 g) each

2 tablespoons fresh lime juice

2 fresh hot chili peppers, stemmed, seeded and finely chopped

6 green (spring) onions, cut on the diagonal into very thin slices, including the green portions

1 tablespoon snipped fresh cilantro (coriander/Chinese parsley)

This popular Mexican dip could not be easier to make. Prepare it just before serving, to keep the color and flavor at their best. If you wish, substitute mild canned green chilies for the fresh hot ones. You can also add 1 or 2 firm, ripe plum (egg) tomatoes that have been seeded and coarsely chopped. Serve the guacamole with fresh vegetables or tortilla or corn chips.

*H*alve the avocados and remove the pits. With a teaspoon scoop out the flesh from the skins and put it into a deep plate. Mash it roughly with a fork, sprinkling with lime juice as you mash.

Quickly mix the chili, green onions and cilantro into the avocado. Serve immediately.

Serves 6

New Potatoes with Tapenade

BOUCHÉES DE POMMES DE TERRE À LA TAPENADE

2 lb (1 kg) small firm-fleshed potatoes, such as red-skinned, Rose fir or White Rose varieties
⅔ cup (5 fl oz/150 ml) water
1 tablespoon fine sea salt

FOR THE TAPENADE:
1 small garlic clove
2 oz (50 g) anchovy fillets in olive oil, well drained
freshly ground pepper
2 tablespoons extra-virgin olive oil
1⅔ tablespoons capers in brine, rinsed and well drained
8 oz (250 g) large plump black olives, pitted

The mild, earthy flavor of boiled potatoes is an ideal backdrop for the Provençal spread called tapenade, a purée of black olives and anchovies. Tapenade is also good spread on toast or served as a condiment with cold roast meats or poultry.

*P*lace the unpeeled potatoes in a small, deep, heavy pot with a tight-fitting lid. Pour in the water and scatter the salt over the top. Cover the pot, place over medium heat and cook for 20 minutes without touching the pot. At this point the potatoes should be cooked and all the water evaporated. To test for doneness, insert the tip of a knife blade into the center of one of the potatoes. Let cool to room temperature.

While the potatoes are cooking, make the tapenade. Pass the garlic clove through a garlic press held over a blender container or the work bowl of a food processor. Add the anchovies, pepper to taste and the oil and process to a fine purée. Add the capers and process again. Add the olives and process quickly once more to form a thick purée.

At serving time, cut the potatoes into thin slices (the skins may be left on) and spread each slice with some of the tapenade. Arrange on a platter.

Serves 8

Artichoke Hearts with Parsley

Coeurs d'Artichauts au Persil

18 small artichokes, about 2½ oz
  (75 g) each
2 lemons, cut in half
4 cups (32 fl oz/1 l) water
½ cup (4 fl oz/100 ml) fresh lemon juice
1 teaspoon coarse salt
½ cup (4 fl oz/100 ml) extra-virgin
  olive oil
2 cloves garlic, cut into thin slivers
1 dried hot chili pepper, crumbled
6 whole cloves
2 pinches of dried oregano
36 fresh parsley leaves

Vegetables prepared in a marinade of olive oil, garlic and oregano are sometimes referred to as à la grecque—"in the Greek style." You can use the same treatment for other firm-textured vegetables such as carrots, broccoli or cauliflower.

Cut off the stems of the artichokes so that only ¾ inch (2 cm) remains. Remove and discard the tough leaves. Cut back the more tender ones to within ¾ inch (2 cm) of the heart. Trim away the tough outer layer covering the hearts and stems, and then rub the artichokes all over with the cut lemon halves.

In a large saucepan bring the water to a boil. Add the lemon juice and coarse salt. Drop in the artichokes and let them cook for 10 minutes; they should still be slightly crunchy. Drain the artichokes and place them, heads down, in a colander to cool.

Pour the oil into a bowl. Add the garlic, chili pepper, cloves and oregano.

When the artichokes are thoroughly drained and cool, add them to the bowl. Mix well and add the parsley. Let stand at room temperature for 1–6 hours.

Arrange the artichokes on an attractive plate and serve with toothpicks.

Serves 6

Curried Vegetables in Filo Packets

ENVELOPPES DE LÉGUMES ÉPICES

3 tablespoons unsalted butter
4 oz (120 g) zucchini (courgettes),
  trimmed and finely chopped
3 oz (100 g) carrots, peeled and finely
  chopped
3 oz (100 g) cultivated (button)
  mushrooms, trimmed and finely
  chopped
2 shallots, finely chopped
2 tablespoons snipped fresh chives
salt
2 teaspoons curry powder
3 tablespoons water
8 oz (250 g) tender heart of green
  cabbage, finely chopped
grated zest of ½ lemon
4 sheets filo pastry

In a large nonstick frying pan, melt 1½ tablespoons of the butter over medium heat. Add the zucchini, carrots, mushrooms, shallots and chives. Cook, stirring, until the vegetables are golden, about 3 minutes. Add salt to taste and the curry powder and cook, stirring, for another 2 minutes. Add the water to the pan and then stir in the cabbage. Cover and cook over low heat, stirring often, for 20 minutes.

Meanwhile, preheat an oven to 425°F (225°C). In a very small pan, melt the remaining 1½ tablespoons butter and let it cool. With a pastry brush butter a nonstick baking sheet very lightly with some of the melted butter.

When the vegetables are cooked, transfer them to a bowl and let them cool a little. Stir in the lemon zest. Cut the filo sheets into quarters; keep the sheets covered with a damp towel to prevent them from drying out. Place a quarter sheet on a work surface and brush the edges with a little of the melted butter, covering a border about 1½ inches (4 cm) wide. Place a large spoonful of the vegetable mixture in the center and spread it into a small rectangle. Fold the sides of the pastry inward and then fold over the top and then the bottom edge, to form a rectangle. Place the packet, seam side down, on the prepared baking sheet. Repeat with the remaining filo sheets and vegetable mixture.

Place the baking sheet in the oven and bake until the pastry is crisp, 12–15 minutes. Serve warm.

Makes 16 small pastry parcels; serves 8

Eggplant Caviar

CAVIAR D'AUBERGINES

2 eggplants (aubergines), 9 oz (300 g)
   each
1 small clove garlic
1½ teaspoons fresh lemon juice
1 tablespoon extra-virgin olive oil
2 or 3 pinches of ground cumin
salt

Puréed roasted eggplant is commonly known as the poor man's caviar, being at once both rich tasting and economical to make. In the Middle East, the spread is also traditionally known as baba ganoosh, *or "harem girl"—no doubt a reference to its seductive texture. Prepare it up to 24 hours in advance. Serve with toasted yogurt quick bread (recipe on page 12), crackers or raw vegetables, and accompany, if you like, with taramasalata (recipe on page 60) or tapenade (recipe on page 42).*

Preheat an oven to 500°F (250°C). With a sharp knife make 2 or 3 slashes in each eggplant so they will not burst as they cook. Place the eggplants on a rack in the oven and position a pan beneath them to catch any drips. Bake until they are black and wrinkled, about 45 minutes. Remove the eggplants from the oven and let them cool until they can be handled.

   Peel the eggplants and place the pulp in a bowl. With a fork mash the pulp to form a coarse consistency. Pass the garlic through a garlic press into the bowl, and then add the lemon juice, olive oil, cumin and salt to taste. Mix well.

   Serve at room temperature.

Serves 4

Onion Tartlets

Tartelettes aux Oignons

13 oz (400 g) pizza dough (*recipe on page 10*)

2 tablespoons extra-virgin olive oil

½ cup (4 fl oz/100 ml) water

½ teaspoon sugar

salt and freshly ground pepper

1 lb (500 g) large onions, thinly sliced and cut into slivers

12 plump black olives, pitted and slivered

12 anchovy fillets in olive oil, drained and cut in half crosswise

⅓ cup (2 oz/50 g) pine nuts

The topping of onions, olives and anchovies is inspired by pissaladière, *the Niçoise relative of the pizza. If you make the tartlets in advance, they may be reheated for 6–8 minutes in a preheated 425°F (225°C) oven.*

*Prepare the pizza dough. Preheat an oven to 500°F (250°C).

On a lightly floured work surface, roll out the dough ⅜ inch (1 cm) thick. With a round pastry cutter 1½ inches (4 cm) in diameter, cut out 24 rounds. Now roll these rounds out again until they are 3/16 inch (.5 cm) thick. Lay the rounds on a nonstick baking sheet.

Combine the oil and water in a medium nonstick frying pan. Add the sugar and salt and pepper to taste. Bring to a boil and add the onions. Cover and cook over gentle heat, stirring from time to time, until the onions are golden and the water evaporates, about 20 minutes. Remove from the heat. Add the olives, anchovies and pine nuts to the onions and mix well.

Divide the filling evenly among the dough rounds. Transfer the baking sheet to the oven and bake until the filling and the edges of the pastry are golden, about 15 minutes. Serve warm.

Makes 24 tartlets; serves 6

Terrine of Mixed Herbs
TERRINE VERTE

1 teaspoon peanut oil or vegetable oil

3 oz (100 g) Swiss chard (silverbeet),
  green leaves only

4 oz (120 g) onions, coarsely cut

3½ oz (100 g) leeks, coarsely cut

1 tablespoon fresh dill leaves

1 tablespoon fresh cilantro (coriander/
  Chinese parsley) leaves

1½ tablespoons fresh parsley leaves

24 fresh mint leaves

24 fresh tarragon leaves

6 sorrel leaves

4 eggs

3 tablespoons ground almonds or
  2 tablespoons natural almond paste

2 tablespoons all-purpose (plain) flour

¼ teaspoon cayenne pepper

salt and freshly ground pepper

A bouquet of fresh herbs combines with deep green Swiss chard and lemony sorrel leaves in this garden-fresh terrine. You may have to visit the local farmer's market to find the herbs, but this exceptional dish is worth the extra effort. If you like, try substituting other herbs or greens such as chives, savory, watercress or arugula (rocket). But make such changes carefully, for the recipe's success depends upon a delicate balance of flavors. The terrine may also be cut into large squares and served as a first course.

$\mathcal{P}$reheat an oven to 300°F (150°C)..Coat the bottom and sides of an 8-inch-square (22-cm) cake pan with the oil; set aside.

Combine the Swiss chard, onions, leeks, dill, cilantro, parsley, mint, tarragon and sorrel in the work bowl of a food processor fitted with a metal blade and process until the herbs are coarsely chopped. Add the eggs, ground almonds or almond paste, flour, cayenne pepper and salt and pepper to taste to the processor bowl and process at high speed until the mixture is well blended. Pour into the prepared pan. Place in the oven and bake until set, about 30 minutes. Remove from the oven and let cool.

Cut into ¾-inch (2-cm) cubes and arrange on a platter. Serve with toothpicks at room temperature.

Serves 8

Marinated Button Mushrooms
CHAMPIGNONS MARINÉS

1 lb (500 g) very small cultivated
  (button) mushrooms
⅔ cup (5 fl oz/150 ml) dry white wine
⅔ cup (5 fl oz/150 ml) rice vinegar
1 teaspoon fine sea salt
1 teaspoon coarsely ground pepper
1 dried hot chili pepper, crumbled
2 teaspoons dried oregano
3 whole cloves
2 tablespoons snipped fresh parsley
1 lemon, thinly sliced, seeded and slices
  cut into quarters
1 small red sweet pepper (capsicum),
  stemmed, seeded, deribbed and cut
  into ⅜-inch (1-cm) squares
1 clove garlic
3 tablespoons extra-virgin olive oil

Rice vinegar, chili pepper and cloves contribute to the spicy-sweet taste these young, tender mushrooms take on during marinating. You can keep the mushrooms in the refrigerator for up to 5 days; they will only gain in flavor. Snipped fresh cilantro (coriander/Chinese parsley) can replace the parsley, in which case 1 tablespoon coriander seed should be added to the marinade.

Select very small mushrooms (no larger than ½ inch/12 mm in diameter). Trim off the stem ends, then wash and pat dry.

Combine the wine and vinegar in a large stainless-steel saucepan. Add the salt, pepper, chili pepper, oregano, cloves, parsley, lemon, sweet pepper and garlic. Bring to a boil and add the mushrooms. Sprinkle them with the oil and boil for 7 minutes. Turn off the heat and let the mixture cool completely before serving.

Serve these mushrooms at room temperature with toothpicks.

Serves 4–6

Smoked Salmon Mousse

MOUSSE DE SAUMON FUMÉ

13–14 oz (400 g) smoked salmon
½ cup (4 oz/120 g) plain yogurt
¼–½ teaspoon cayenne pepper
½ teaspoon paprika
2 tablespoons extra-virgin olive oil
1 lemon

Most savory mousses are rich in cream, but this version has a lighter flavor and consistency because it is made with yogurt, olive oil and lemon juice. It may be prepared up to 24 hours in advance and stored in the refrigerator. Serve with coarse country bread, thinly sliced rye bread, blini (recipe on page 12) or sticks of raw vegetable.

Roughly chop half of the smoked salmon and put it into the work bowl of a food processor. Add the yogurt, cayenne, paprika and olive oil. Grate the zest of the lemon into the processor bowl, then halve the lemon, squeeze it and measure 2 tablespoons juice. Add the juice to the bowl and process the ingredients for as long as necessary to form a thin purée.

Transfer the purée to a large bowl. Coarsely chop the remaining salmon and add it to the purée. Mix well, cover and refrigerate until serving time.

Serves 8

Seafood Tempura

TEMPURA MARINE

12 large shrimp (prawns) in the shell,
    each weighing about 2½ oz (75 g) if
    heads intact
12 sea scallops
¾ cup (6 fl oz/175 ml) very cold water
1 egg yolk
1 cup (4 oz/120 g) all-purpose (plain)
    flour, plus extra for dusting the
    shellfish
salt
peanut oil or vegetable oil for deep-frying
lemon wedges

*Lacy, crisp tempura batter coats fresh scallops and shrimp
in this classic Japanese preparation.*

*I*f you have purchased shrimp with their heads, cut off and
discard the heads. Peel the shrimp, leaving the shell ring
nearest the tail intact. Make a very shallow slit along the
outside curve of the body of each shrimp and remove and
discard the dark intestinal vein. Make shallow parallel cuts
along the inside curve of each shrimp so they will not curl
during cooking. Slice each scallop in half horizontally to
form 2 rounds.

To make the batter, pour the water into a bowl. Add the
egg yolk and whisk rapidly with a fork. Quickly whisk in
the flour and then salt to taste. Do not beat too long.

Pour the oil into a deep-fat fryer or a heavy saucepan to a
depth of at least 2 inches (5 cm). Heat the oil over medium
heat until it reaches 350°F (180°C), or until a small bit of
bread tossed into the oil surfaces immediately. When the
oil is ready, lightly flour the shrimp and scallops, dip them
into the batter and then, 5 or 6 pieces at a time, carefully
slip them into the oil; be careful not to crowd the pan.
Cook, turning them with a slotted utensil, until lightly
golden; the scallops will take 2 minutes and the shrimp will
take 3 minutes. Remove with a slotted utensil to paper
towels to drain briefly. Arrange the shrimp and scallops on
a serving dish and serve at once with the lemon wedges.

Serves 6–8

Greek-Style Caviar Spread
TARAMASALATA

13 oz (400 g) tarama
¾ cup (6 oz/200 g) plain yogurt
grated zest of 1 lemon
2 tablespoons fresh lemon juice
⅓ cup (2 oz/50 g) fine dry bread
  crumbs
3 tablespoons extra-virgin olive oil
¼ teaspoon paprika
4–6 pinches of cayenne pepper

A rich and aromatic purée based on salted cod roe, or tarama, this spread is one of the best-known of the Greek appetizers, which are called meze. *Serve it on vegetable slices, scoop it with fingers of oven-crisped pita bread, or spread it atop blini (recipe on page 12)—just as caviar is sometimes served. The tarama can be purchased in bulk or in jars from well-stocked supermarkets or Greek and Middle Eastern shops. Gray mullet tarama may be used as well.*

*P*lace the tarama in the work bowl of a food processor fitted with a metal blade or in a blender. Add the yogurt, lemon zest and juice, bread crumbs, olive oil, paprika and cayenne pepper. Process until you have a smooth purée.

  Transfer to a bowl and serve at room temperature or chilled.

Serves 8

Gravlax with Mustard Sauce
SAUMON MARINÉ, SAUCE MOUTARDE

2 fresh salmon fillets of the same size
with skin intact, about 3 lb (1.5 kg)
total weight, all scales removed

¼ cup (2 oz/60 g) coarse sea salt

¼ cup (2 oz/60 g) superfine (caster)
sugar

2 tablespoons crushed white
peppercorns

2 large bunches fresh dill

FOR THE SAUCE:

6 tablespoons (3 oz/90 g) Dijon mustard

2 teaspoons superfine (caster) sugar

6 tablespoons (3 fl oz/100 ml) white
wine vinegar

1⅔ cups (13 fl oz/200 ml) peanut oil or
vegetable oil

2 tablespoons snipped fresh dill

*P*at the fillets dry with paper towels. In a small bowl mix together the salt, sugar and peppercorns. Place 5 of the dill sprigs on the bottom of a shallow baking dish. Lay one of the salmon fillets on top, skin side down. Sprinkle with half of the salt mixture and top with all but 5 of the remaining dill sprigs. Sprinkle with the remaining salt mixture and place the second piece of salmon, skin side up, atop the first. Lay the 5 remaining dill sprigs on top.

Place a plate on top of the salmon and set a weight (about 2 lb/1 kg) on top. Cover and refrigerate for 36 hours, turning them over every 12 hours and draining off any liquid in the dish. At the end of this time, rinse the fillets several times under cold water and pat dry with paper towels. Place the fillets skin side down on a work surface and cut on the diagonal across the grain into thin slices without cutting into the skin; the salmon should appear as if it is still a whole fillet. Refrigerate the salmon while you make the sauce.

In a small bowl stir together the mustard, sugar and vinegar. Gradually add the oil in a thin, steady stream, beating with a whisk or an electric beater until you have a fully emulsified sauce. Stir in the snipped dill and pour into a sauce dish.

Guests should dip the salmon in the sauce before eating.

Serves 10

Mussels in Spicy Vinaigrette

Moules en Vinaigrette Pimentée

6 lb (3 kg) mussels in the shell

¼ cup (2 fl oz/60 ml) extra-virgin olive oil

¼ cup (2 fl oz/60 ml) good-quality red wine vinegar

1 teaspoon sweet paprika

1 teaspoon hot paprika

1 large lemon, cut into slices ¹⁄₁₆ inch (2 mm) thick, seeded and slices cut into sixths

2 cloves garlic, finely chopped

2 tablespoons snipped fresh parsley

salt

Try this simple first course when mussels are in the market. The blend of sweet and hot paprikas in the vinaigrette complements the sea-fresh flavor of the shellfish. You can also use good-sized fresh clams.

Scrub the mussels and remove and discard their beards. Rinse them under cold water and drain well.

Pour the oil and vinegar into a large stockpot. Add the sweet and hot paprikas, lemon pieces, garlic, parsley and salt to taste. Bring to a boil and simmer for 1 minute. Add the mussels, cover and cook until the mussels open, 3–4 minutes.

Transfer the mussels and their cooking liquid to a deep plate, discarding any that have not opened. Let cool to room temperature and then refrigerate for 2–4 hours before serving.

Serves 4–6

Endive Boats with Smoked Salmon Stuffing

BARQUETTES D'ENDIVES AU SAUMON

6 oz (200 g) smoked salmon, roughly
  chopped
2 tablespoons extra-virgin olive oil
1 tablespoon fresh lemon juice
2 tablespoons snipped fresh chives
salt and freshly ground pepper
4 large Belgian endives (witloof/chicory)
1 oz (20 g) salmon roe

Devotees of smoked salmon say you need little more than a squeeze of lemon and some chives to highlight its flavor. True to that spirit, this recipe serves the lightly seasoned salmon nestled in endive spears—crisp boat-shaped containers with a refreshing hint of bitterness that further complements the seafood.

Combine the smoked salmon, olive oil, lemon juice, chives and salt and pepper to taste in a bowl. Stir until well blended. Cover and marinate in the refrigerator for 1 hour.

Remove the outer leaves of the endives (reserve for another use). Separate from the heart the tender leaves that are large enough for stuffing. There should be 6–8 leaves from each endive. Chill in the refrigerator.

At serving time, gently stir the salmon roe into the smoked salmon mixture. Spoon the salmon mixture into the endive leaves, or "boats," and arrange on a platter. Serve at once.

Serves 8–10

Fish Tartare

Tartare de Poissons

6 oz (200 g) white fish fillets such as sea
   bream, sea bass, cod, sole, halibut or
   flounder
6 oz (200 g) salmon fillets
salt and freshly ground pepper
3 tablespoons extra-virgin olive oil

It is interesting to note the similarity in concept between a classic French tartare and the ever-more-popular Japanese sashimi: both present with utmost simplicity the flavor and texture of the freshest seafood. You can use any firm, white-fleshed fish, but be certain that it has never been frozen and is very fresh. Prepare the tartare as close to serving time as possible, and no more than 2–3 hours ahead, keeping it covered in the refrigerator. Serve with toasted bread—rubbed with garlic, if you like—and with such garnishes as olives, sliced green (spring) onions, capers, chopped gherkins and lemon wedges.

Cut the white fish and salmon into long, thin strips. Place the strips in a bowl nested in a larger bowl filled with ice cubes. Add a generous amount of salt and pepper and mix thoroughly. Sprinkle with the olive oil and mix again.

Transfer the fish to a deep plate, cover and refrigerate until serving time.

Serves 4

Ceviche

1¼ lb (600 g) white fish fillets
  (see note, right)
juice of 5–6 limes
2 firm but ripe tomatoes, peeled, seeded
  and cut into small dice
1 small fresh pimiento or other sweet
  pepper, stemmed, seeded, deribbed
  and chopped
1 green (spring) onion, chopped,
  including the green portions
6 tablespoons (1½ oz/45 g) snipped
  fresh cilantro (coriander/Chinese
  parsley)
salt and freshly ground pepper
1 avocado, pitted, peeled and cut into
  small dice
10 black olives, pitted
1 teaspoon dried oregano

The acidity of fresh lime juice "cooks" the raw seafood in this well-known Latin American appetizer. Use any firm, white-fleshed fish such as sea bream, sea bass, cod, sole, halibut or flounder. If you want more spice, add a small chili pepper — stemmed, seeded and chopped. While only several hours of marinating are necessary, you can refrigerate the ceviche for up to 12 hours in advance. Serve alone or with toast.

Cut the fish fillets into ⅜-inch (1-cm) dice and put them into a large porcelain bowl. Pour the lime juice over the fish, making sure all the pieces are covered. Let stand for 3–4 hours.

Drain the fish cubes and pat dry on paper towels. Put the fish cubes into a large bowl and add the tomatoes, sweet pepper, green onion, cilantro and salt and pepper to taste. Stir to blend and refrigerate for at least 2 hours.

At serving time, dice the avocado as directed and stir it into the fish mixture, along with the olives and oregano. Serve at once.

Serves 6

Parslied Crab with Hard-Cooked Eggs

Crabe Persillé aux Oeufs Durs

1 tablespoon (¼ oz/7 g) unflavored
  gelatin (1 envelope)
1⅔ cups (13 fl oz/400 ml) water
3 tablespoons dark rum
13 oz (400 g) cooked fresh crab meat
¼ cup (1 oz/30 g) chopped fresh parsley
4 pinches of cayenne pepper
salt and freshly ground pepper
2 eggs, hard-cooked
1 lime

Lime zest and rum give an exotic Caribbean flavor to this delectable crab meat presentation. Guacamole (recipe on page 41) makes an excellent companion.

*I*n a small bowl sprinkle the gelatin over ⅓ cup (3 fl oz/ 80 ml) of the water and let stand for about 3 minutes.

In a saucepan bring the remaining water to a boil and remove from the heat. Stir in the rum and the softened gelatin. Let cool until thick and syrupy. Meanwhile, flake the crab meat into a large bowl, not too finely. Mix in the parsley, cayenne and salt and pepper to taste.

Shell the eggs and cut in half. Remove the yolks, put them in a stainless-steel fine-mesh strainer held over the bowl and, with the back of a spoon, force the yolks through the strainer. Finely dice the whites and add to the bowl. Finally, grate the zest from the lime directly into the bowl. Mix well. Stir in the thickened gelatin mixture. Line a shallow 7-inch (20-cm) dish with plastic wrap. Pour the crab mixture into the prepared dish, smooth the surface, cover and refrigerate for 4 hours.

At serving time, invert the dish onto a serving plate. Lift off the dish and then peel off the plastic wrap. Cut into ¾-inch (2-cm) cubes to serve.

Serves 6–8

Sesame Shrimp

CREVETTES FRITES AU SÉSAME

24 large shrimp (prawns) in the shell
2 egg whites
3 tablespoons sesame seed
peanut oil or vegetable oil for deep-frying

Fried butterflied shrimp get a crisp, rich coating from sesame seeds—a traditional Chinese treatment. If you like, serve the shrimp with the sweet-and-sour dipping sauce on page 20. You can also coat and cook thin strips of boned and skinned chicken breast in the same way.

Peel the shrimp, leaving the shell ring nearest the tail intact. With a sharp knife slit each shrimp along the outside curve of the body, cutting three fourths of the way through. Remove and discard the dark intestinal vein. Flatten the shrimp, which will open out into a V-shape.

In a bowl, beat the egg whites with a fork until frothy. Put the sesame seed in another bowl.

Pour the oil into a deep-fat fryer or heavy saucepan to a depth of at least 2 inches (5 cm). Place the pan over medium heat until the oil reaches 350°F (180°C), or until a small bit of bread tossed into the oil surfaces immediately. When the oil is ready, dip the shrimp first in the egg white, and then roll them in the sesame seed. Being careful not to crowd the pan, drop 5 or 6 shrimp into the hot oil and cook, turning them with a slotted spoon, until golden brown, 2–3 minutes.

Using the slotted spoon, transfer the shrimp to paper towels to drain. Repeat with the remaining shrimp. Serve hot, warm or at room temperature.

Serves 6

Curried Sardine Mousse

MOUSSE DE SARDINES AU CURRY

8 boned and skinned canned sardines in
   olive oil, well drained and tails
   discarded
6 oz (200 g) fresh cheese such as ricotta
   or mascarpone, well drained
1 teaspoon curry powder
2 tablespoons snipped fresh parsley
¼ cup (2 oz/60 g) capers in brine, rinsed
   and well drained
1 tablespoon anchovy paste
pinch of freshly grated lemon zest

*The robust flavor of canned sardines stands up well to the
complex taste of curry powder; soft, creamy cheese enriches
the mixture and gives it a smooth consistency. If you like, you
can leave out the anchovy paste. Spread the mousse on toast,
hard-cooked eggs or cherry tomatoes.*

*I*n the work bowl of a food processor, combine the
sardines, cheese, curry powder, parsley, capers, anchovy
paste and lemon zest. Process, using short pulses, until a
coarse mousselike texture forms.

   Transfer the mousse to a serving bowl and serve at room
temperature.

Serves 8

Potted Smoked Trout
RILLETTES DE TRUITE FUMÉE

4 teaspoons (⅓ oz/10 g) unflavored
   gelatin (1⅓ envelopes)
1⅔ cups (13 fl oz/400 ml) vegetable,
   fish or chicken stock
2 tablespoons fresh lemon juice
1 teaspoon crushed peppercorns
4–6 pinches of cayenne pepper
1¼ lb (600 g) smoked trout fillets
¼ cup (1 oz/30 g) snipped fresh dill

Mixed with a jellied bouillon, smoked trout becomes smooth and spreadable, a texture that complements its rich flavor. You'll find smoked trout at good-quality delicatessens and seafood shops; if you like, try using smoked mackerel in its place. Serve on thinly sliced cucumber rounds, rye bread, toast or blini (recipe on page 12).

In a small bowl sprinkle the gelatin over ⅓ cup (3 fl oz/ 80 ml) of the stock and let stand for about 3 minutes, to soften.

Meanwhile, in a saucepan combine the lemon juice, peppercorns and cayenne pepper and stir well. Stir in the remaining 1⅓ cups (10 fl oz/320 ml) stock. Bring to a boil and remove from the heat. Stir in the softened gelatin, cover and refrigerate until the mixture begins to become syrupy and thick, about 30 minutes.

While the gelatin mixture is thickening, remove the skin and bones from the trout fillets. Break up the flesh very finely and add to the syrupy gelatin mixture, mixing well. Then stir in the dill and refrigerate until the mixture sets to a thick, spreadable consistency. Serve chilled.

Serves 8

Cold Veal with Tuna Mayonnaise

VEAU À LA SAUCE AU THON

8 cups (64 fl oz/2 l) water
2 small carrots, trimmed
2 celery stalks with leaves, trimmed
1 onion studded with 2 whole cloves
2 fresh parsley sprigs
1 bay leaf
2 teaspoons coarse sea salt
½ teaspoon whole black peppercorns
½ teaspoon whole white peppercorns
3 lb (1.5 kg) boned rolled veal

FOR THE SAUCE:
1 egg yolk
1 teaspoon mild mustard
pinch of salt
½ cup (4 fl oz/125 ml) peanut oil or
    vegetable oil
1 tablespoon fresh lemon juice
4 oz (125 g) canned tuna in olive oil,
    well drained
2 teaspoons anchovy paste
2 pinches of freshly grated nutmeg
freshly ground pepper
1 tablespoon heavy (double) cream

1 tablespoon capers in brine, rinsed and
    well drained

*This classic Italian first course—*vitello tonnato—*pairs cold poached veal with a smooth mayonnaise-based sauce flavored with tuna and anchovies.*

Combine the water, carrots, celery, clove-studded onion, parsley, bay leaf, coarse salt and peppercorns in an oval dutch oven or other heavy pot. Bring to a boil. Add the meat, cover with a tight-fitting lid and simmer for 1½ hours.

Remove the pot from the heat and let the meat cool in the cooking liquid. When it is cold, remove it from the liquid and wrap it in plastic wrap. Refrigerate for at least 8 hours.

To make the sauce, combine the egg yolk and mustard in a blender. Process briefly to blend. Add the salt and let rest for 1 minute. With the motor running, slowly pour the oil into the yolk mixture in a thin, steady stream. The mixture will be quite thick. Mix in the lemon juice. Transfer to a bowl and set aside.

Place the tuna, anchovy paste, nutmeg and pepper in the clean blender container; blend to a smooth purée. Add the mustard mixture and blend just until combined. Add the cream and blend for another 10 seconds. Transfer to a bowl, cover and refrigerate for up to 6 hours.

To serve, cut the veal against the grain into slices about ⅛ inch (3 mm) thick. Arrange on a serving platter. Spoon the sauce over the top and garnish with capers.

Serves 6–8

Lamb Tikka

AGNEAU TIKKA

1½–2 lb (800 g–1 kg) boneless lamb
   leg, cut into 1-inch (2.5-cm) cubes
1 clove garlic, cut into quarters
   lengthwise
1 onion, cut into quarters
1 tablespoon grated fresh ginger
½ cup (4 fl oz/100 ml) plain
   yogurt
3 tablespoons fresh lemon juice
1 teaspoon ground cumin
1 teaspoon ground turmeric
1 tablespoon garam masala
1 tablespoon snipped fresh mint
1 tablespoon snipped fresh cilantro
   (coriander/Chinese parsley)
1 teaspoon salt

A variation on Indian tandoori cooking (see page 92), tikka-style foods are cut into bite-sized chunks for marinating and grilling. Lamb, used here, is a favorite; chunks of boneless, skinless chicken breast are also good. Serve with crisp vegetables such as chunks of cucumber, radishes or hearts of lettuce.

Place the lamb in a bowl. Put the garlic, onion, ginger, yogurt, lemon juice, cumin, turmeric, garam masala, mint, cilantro and salt into a blender and whirl until you have a smooth mixture. Pour the yogurt mixture over the lamb and mix thoroughly so that each piece of meat is evenly coated. Cover and refrigerate for 6–8 hours. If using bamboo skewers, soak the skewers in water to cover for 30 minutes.

Preheat a broiler (griller). Line a baking sheet with aluminum foil and lightly oil it. Thread 3 lamb cubes onto each small bamboo or metal skewer and lay the skewers on the baking sheet. Place the sheet about 2 inches (5 cm) from the heat and broil (grill) the meat, turning once, until tender but still pink, about 5 minutes on each side.

Serves 6

Chicken Bouchées with Soy Sauce

BOUCHÉES DE POULET À LA SAUCE DE SOJA

1½ lb (750 g) chicken or turkey meat, cut into ¾-inch (2-cm) dice
8 tablespoons (4 fl oz/125 ml) soy sauce
4 tablespoons (2 fl oz/60 ml) muscat or other sweet white wine
1 teaspoon Chinese five-spice powder
salt and freshly ground pepper
6 tablespoons (3 fl oz/90 ml) dry white vermouth
4 tablespoons (2 fl oz/60 ml) peanut oil or vegetable oil

*I*n the work bowl of a food processor fitted with a metal blade, combine the chicken or turkey, 2 tablespoons of the soy sauce, 2 tablespoons of the muscat, the five-spice powder and salt and pepper to taste. Process at medium speed until it forms a fine texture, about 1 minute.

Shape the mixture into walnut-sized balls by rolling a small amount between your palms. To make forming the balls easier, dampen your hands with cold water.

In a small bowl stir together the remaining muscat, the remaining soy sauce and the vermouth.

Heat 2 tablespoons of the oil in a large nonstick frying pan over medium heat. Arrange half of the meatballs in the pan and cook until golden brown, 10–15 minutes. Every now and again, move the pan in a smooth, circular motion so that the balls will turn to cook on all sides without danger of breaking. Remove the meatballs to a plate. Add the remaining 2 tablespoons oil to the pan and cook the remaining meatballs in the same manner.

Remove the meatballs to the plate and discard the oil from the pan. Pour the soy-wine mixture into the pan and return all the meatballs to the pan. Cook over high heat, moving the pan in a circular motion, until all of the sauce evaporates and the meatballs are coated with an amber glaze.

Transfer the meatballs to a deep plate and serve hot, warm or at room temperature.

Serves 6

Pork and Celeriac Terrine

Terrine de Porc au Céleri

1 tablespoon peanut oil or vegetable oil

1¼ lb (600 g) pork loin

5 oz (150 g) cooked ham, roughly chopped

3 oz (100 g) white bread without crust, roughly chopped, about 1½ cups

1 oz (30 g) dried porcini, soaked in hot water to cover until softened and drained

1 tablespoon snipped fresh parsley

2 eggs

3 cloves garlic

salt

1 teaspoon crushed peppercorns

¼ teaspoon freshly grated nutmeg

1 medium celeriac (celery root), about 8 oz (250 g)

1 apple

1 teaspoon superfine (caster) sugar

Celeriac, dried mushrooms and apple complement pork fillet and ham in this hearty French terrine.

Preheat an oven to 300°F (150°C). Use some of the oil to oil a terrine or loaf pan. Set aside.

Roughly chop half of the pork and place it in the work bowl of a food processor fitted with a metal blade. Add the ham, bread and drained mushrooms and process for 2 minutes. Add the parsley and eggs, and then pass the garlic through a garlic press held over the work bowl. Process for another 2 minutes. Transfer the mixture to a large bowl.

Cut the remaining meat into ⅜-inch (1-cm) dice and add to the bowl. Add salt to taste, peppercorns and nutmeg and mix thoroughly. Peel the celeriac. Halve the apple lengthwise and peel one half of it. Grate together the celeriac and the peeled apple half, using the matchstick-cut grating disk in the food processor. Add this mixture to the bowl holding the other ingredients and mix thoroughly.

Pack the pork mixture into the prepared terrine and press down well. Lightly brush the remaining oil over the surface. Slice the remaining apple half into thin semicircles and lay them on top, slightly overlapping. Sprinkle evenly with the sugar and put the terrine into the oven. When it has cooked for 1 hour, reduce the heat to 250°F (125°C) and cook for 45 minutes longer.

Remove from the oven and let cool to room temperature. To serve, cut into slices.

Serves 8

Carpaccio

1¼ lb (600 g) beef fillet, sirloin or round, about 2½ inches (6 cm) thick, trimmed of all fat, rolled and tied

FOR THE SAUCE:
1 egg yolk
2 teaspoons mustard
pinch of salt
¾ cup (6 fl oz/180 ml) peanut oil or vegetable oil
2 tablespoons heavy (double) cream
1 tablespoon Worcestershire sauce
1 teaspoon Cognac or other brandy

Prime beef is sliced to near-translucent thinness in this recipe, which originated at Harry's Bar in Venice, Italy. The subtle colors of the beef on its white platter are said to evoke the beautiful Venetian sunsets painted by Vittore Carpaccio. If you like, add a little anchovy paste to the sauce.

*P*lace the meat in a plastic freezer bag and place the bag in the freezer for 1 hour. At the end of this time the meat will be very firm and easy to cut into thin slices.

Meanwhile, prepare the sauce. Combine the egg yolk and mustard in a blender or food processor fitted with a metal blade. Process briefly to blend. Add the salt and let rest for 1 minute. With the motor running, slowly pour the oil into the yolk mixture in a thin, steady stream. The mixture will be quite thick. Mix in the cream, Worcestershire sauce and brandy. Cover and refrigerate.

When the meat is chilled, remove it from the bag and place it on a board. Cut the bag open along one side and the closed end so that you have one large sheet. Spread the sheet over your work surface. Snip off the string and slice the meat ⅛ inch (3 mm) thick and place the slices in pairs, side-by-side, on half of the plastic sheet. Fold the uncovered portion of the sheet over the meat and, using a rolling pin, gently roll over the meat to flatten the slices. They will quickly become translucent.

Cover a platter with the meat slices. With the aid of a spoon, drizzle the sauce over the meat in a zigzag pattern.

Serves 6

Pork Meatballs with Peanuts

Boulettes Cacahuetes

1¼ lb (600 g) pork loin, cut into
 ¾-inch (2-cm) dice
½ cup (3 oz/100 g) shelled raw peanuts
6 fresh mint sprigs, stemmed
6 fresh cilantro (coriander/Chinese
 parsley) sprigs, stemmed
2 egg whites
2 teaspoons Chinese five-spice powder
salt
4 tablespoons (2 fl oz/60 ml) peanut oil
 or vegetable oil

Chopped peanuts, mint, cilantro and Chinese five-spice powder impart a wonderfully exotic accent to these meatballs. The mixture also works well with lamb or beef. Accompany with matchsticks of cucumber, small whole green (spring) onions or wedges of fresh fruit. If you'd like a dipping sauce, mix soy sauce with a squeeze of lemon, or try the sweet-and-sour sauce on page 20.

*I*n the work bowl of a food processor fitted with a metal blade, combine the pork, peanuts, mint, cilantro, egg whites, five-spice powder and salt to taste. Process only until the mixture forms a not-too-fine texture.

Shape the pork mixture into balls the size of a walnut by rolling a small amount of the mixture between your palms to form each one. To make forming the balls easier, dip your hands into cold water before you begin to shape each ball.

Heat 2 tablespoons of the oil in a large nonstick frying pan over medium heat. Arrange half of the meatballs in the pan and cook until golden brown, about 10 minutes. Every now and again, move the pan in a smooth, circular motion so that the balls will turn to cook on all sides without danger of breaking. Remove the meatballs to a serving plate. Add the remaining 2 tablespoons oil to the pan and cook the remaining meatballs in the same manner.

Serve the meatballs hot, warm or at room temperature.

Serves 8

Tandoori-Style Chicken

POULET TANDOORI

1 chicken, about 3½ lb (1.7 kg)
¼ cup (2 fl oz/60 ml) fresh lemon juice
1 clove garlic
¾ cup (7 oz/200 ml) plain yogurt
1 tablespoon sweet paprika
1 teaspoon ground cumin
1 teaspoon ground ginger
½ teaspoon ground cinnamon
½ teaspoon ground cloves
½ teaspoon freshly grated nutmeg
½ teaspoon ground cardamom
½ teaspoon freshly ground pepper
1 teaspoon fine sea salt

In this recipe, tandoori-style spices flavor oven-baked chicken. Serve with slices of tomato, cucumber and radish and a selection of chutneys. If you like, wrap the chicken in thin, soft Indian breads such as nan, roti or paratha.

Cut the chicken into 8 pieces and remove the skin. With a sharp knife make several deep parallel cuts about ¾ inch (2 cm) apart in each piece of meat, cutting against the grain.

Put the chicken pieces into a deep plate and sprinkle with the lemon juice. Let stand for 15 minutes, turning each piece two or three times.

Meanwhile, pass the garlic through a garlic press held over a small bowl. Add the yogurt and all the spices and stir together. Pour this mixture over the chicken and mix well. Cover and refrigerate for 8 hours, turning two or three times.

About 1 hour before serving time, remove the chicken from the refrigerator. Transfer the chicken pieces from the marinade to an oven rack, reserving the marinade. Line a baking sheet with aluminum foil and position it in the oven under where the rack will be, to catch any drips. Alternatively, place a rack in a roasting pan and arrange the chicken pieces on the rack. About 15 minutes before you wish to cook the chicken, preheat the oven to 500°F (250°C). When the oven is hot, put the chicken in it and cook until tender, about 35 minutes, turning the pieces after about 15 minutes and basting them with the reserved marinade three or four times. Serve hot.

Serves 8

Beef Meatballs with Parmesan

BOULETTES AU PARMESAN ET AU PERSIL

1½ lb (700 g) lean ground (minced) beef
salt and freshly ground pepper
4 pinches of freshly grated nutmeg
½ cup (2 oz/70 g) freshly grated Parmesan cheese
¼ cup (1½ oz/45 g) snipped fresh parsley
4 tablespoons (2 fl oz/ 60 ml) extra-virgin olive oil

If you've ever wondered why Italian meatballs have so much flavor, one of the secrets—revealed here—is the addition of Parmesan cheese. You can substitute pork or veal for part or all of the beef. For a different presentation, thread the meatballs on tiny skewers after cooking.

*P*ut the beef into a bowl and season with a small amount of salt and plenty of pepper. Add the nutmeg, Parmesan cheese and parsley. Knead the ingredients together with your hands until thoroughly mixed.

Shape the meat mixture into balls the size of a walnut by rolling a small amount of the mixture between your palms to form each one. To make forming the balls easier, dip your hands into cold water before you begin to shape each ball.

Heat 2 tablespoons of the olive oil in a large nonstick frying pan over medium heat. Arrange half the meatballs in the pan and cook until golden brown, about 5 minutes. Every now and again, move the pan around in a smooth, circular motion so that the balls will turn to cook on all sides without danger of breaking. Remove the meatballs to a serving plate. Add the remaining 2 tablespoons oil to the pan and cook the remaining meatballs in the same manner.

Serve the meatballs hot, warm or at room temperature.

Serves 6–8

Mini Pizzas with Spicy Meat Topping

Mini Pizzas à la Viande

13 oz (400 g) pizza dough (recipe on page 10)

2 tablespoons extra-virgin olive oil

8 oz (250 g) onions, chopped, about 2 cups

1 lb (500 g) lean ground (minced) beef

3 tablespoons tomato paste

1 teaspoon superfine (caster) sugar

1 teaspoon ground cumin

1 teaspoon sweet paprika

½ teaspoon cayenne pepper

salt

A subtly spiced mixture of lean ground beef tops little rounds of pizza dough. If you make the pizzas in advance, reheat them in a 425°F (225°C) oven for 6–8 minutes.

Preheat an oven to 500°F (250°C). On a lightly floured work surface, roll out the dough ⅜ inch (1 cm) thick. With a round pastry cutter 1½ inches (4 cm) in diameter, cut out 24 rounds. Now roll these rounds out again until they are ³⁄₁₆ inch (.5 cm) thick. Lay the rounds on a nonstick baking sheet.

Heat the oil in a medium nonstick frying pan over medium heat. Add the onions and fry, stirring constantly, until they are golden, about 5 minutes. Add the meat, tomato paste, sugar, cumin, paprika, cayenne pepper and salt to taste. Cook over high heat, stirring constantly, for 5 minutes. Remove from the heat and let cool to room temperature.

Divide the beef mixture evenly among the dough rounds. Transfer the baking sheet to the oven and bake the pizzas until the crusts are golden, about 15 minutes. Serve warm.

Makes 24 mini pizzas; serves 8

Beef and Currant Rolls

PETITS ROULEAUX AU BOEUF

3 tablespoons peanut oil or vegetable oil
6 oz (200 g) onions, finely chopped, about 1½ cups
13 oz (400 g) lean ground (minced) beef
salt and freshly ground pepper
⅓ cup (2 oz/50 g) sliced almonds, lightly toasted
⅓ cup (2 oz/50 g) pine nuts, lightly toasted
⅓ cup (2 oz/50 g) dried currants
2 tablespoons snipped fresh parsley
6 sheets filo pastry

Crisp filo dough encases a savory-sweet mixture of lean ground beef, currants, pine nuts and almonds. The filo sheets can be folded into triangles instead of rolls.

*P*reheat an oven to 425°F (225°C). Heat 1 tablespoon of the oil in a medium nonstick frying pan over medium heat. Add the onions and fry, stirring, until golden, about 5 minutes. Add the meat and 1 tablespoon of the oil to the pan and cook, breaking up the meat, until lightly browned, 3–4 minutes. Season to taste with salt and pepper.

Transfer the meat mixture to a bowl and add the almonds, pine nuts, currants and parsley. Mix thoroughly.

Cut the filo sheets in half crosswise. Place a half sheet on a work surface; cover the remaining sheets with a damp towel so they do not dry out. On half of the sheet, spread one-twelfth of the meat mixture in a rectangle about 3 inches (7.5 cm) long and ¾ inch (2 cm) wide, leaving the bottom edge and sides uncovered. Fold the bottom edge over the mixture, then fold in the sides and roll up the pastry. Repeat with the remaining ingredients.

Using a pastry brush, oil a large baking sheet with some of the remaining oil. Arrange the rolls on the baking sheet at least ⅜ inch (1 cm) apart. Lightly brush the pastry with the remaining oil.

Bake until golden and crisp, 18–20 minutes. Serve while still crisp, either hot or warm.

Makes 12 rolls; serves 6

Caramelized Pork Fillet

FILET DE PORC CARAMELISÉ

¼ cup (3 oz/90 g) orange blossom
  honey
2 tablespoons rice vinegar
2 tablespoons dry vermouth
1 teaspoon fish sauce
½ teaspoon Chinese five-spice powder
2 pork fillets, about 1 lb (450 g) each
salt and freshly ground pepper
2 tablespoons peanut oil or vegetable oil

The sweet-salty mixture of honey, vermouth and fish sauce—a Southeast Asian seasoning and condiment available in Thai and Vietnamese markets and well-stocked supermarkets—points up the natural sweetness of pork in this satisfying appetizer. Serve cold, thinly sliced, accompanied by slivers of fresh cucumber.

*P*our the honey, vinegar, vermouth and fish sauce into a small bowl and add the five-spice powder. Mix thoroughly. Sprinkle the pork fillets with salt and pepper to taste.

In an oval dutch oven or other heavy pot just large enough to hold the meat, heat the oil over medium heat. Add the fillets and cook, turning, until browned on all sides, 7–8 minutes. Remove the fillets to a plate.

Discard the cooking oil and pour the honey mixture into the pot. Place over medium heat and stir, scraping up any browned bits stuck to the bottom, for 4–5 minutes. Return the meat to the pot, cover with a tight-fitting lid and cook over low heat, turning often, until tender, about 30 minutes.

Remove the meat to a plate. Reduce the cooking liquid over high heat until it caramelizes, about 5 minutes. Remove the pot from the heat and return the fillets to the pot. Turn them in the reduced sauce until they are well coated and then transfer them to the plate. Let cool.

To serve, cut the fillets against the grain into thin slices and arrange on a platter.

Serves 6

Chinese Spareribs

TRAVERS DE PORC À LA CHINOISE

2½ lb (1.2 kg) pork spareribs, cut into
   pieces 1¼ inches (3 cm) long
¼ cup (3 oz/90 g) honey
2 tablespoons soy sauce
2 tablespoons dry sherry
1 teaspoon Chinese five-spice powder
1 teaspoon ground Sichuan pepper

Ask your butcher to cut the spareribs into bite-sized pieces. These aromatic ribs are frequently served as part of the Chinese midday meal known as dim sum. Accompany with fresh, crisp vegetables such as green (spring) onions or radishes.

*Place the spareribs in a shallow dish. In a small bowl stir together the honey, soy sauce, sherry, five-spice powder and Sichuan pepper. Add the honey mixture to the spareribs and mix until the ribs are well coated. Let stand for 1 hour.

Preheat an oven to 300°F (150°C). Arrange the spareribs in a single layer on a nonstick baking sheet. Place them in the oven and cook until tender, about 1 hour, turning them over halfway through the cooking time.

Serve hot, warm or at room temperature.

Serves 8

Glossary

The following glossary defines terms specifically as they relate to hors d'oeuvres and appetizers. Included are major and unusual ingredients and basic techniques.

ALMOND PASTE, NATURAL
A thick, unsweetened paste of ground almonds that enhances the body and flavor of first-course fillings and spreads. Resembling marzipan in consistency, it is found in specialty-food shops or in the baking or confectionery section of well-stocked supermarkets.

ALMONDS
With their mellow, sweet flavor, almonds are used often as an ingredient or garnish in hors d'oeuvres and appetizers. Sliced almonds are sold prepackaged in supermarkets. Toasting develops their flavor: Spread them in a single layer on a baking sheet and heat in a 250°F (120°C) oven until golden, 8–10 minutes, watching carefully to guard against burning. Ground to a fine powder, almonds add body and flavor to first-course fillings and spreads.

ANCHOVIES
Tiny saltwater fish, related to sardines, most commonly used as canned fillets that have been salted and preserved in oil. Imported anchovy fillets packed in olive oil are the most commonly available; those packed in salt, available canned in some Italian delicatessens, are considered the finest. Smooth pastes made from preserved anchovy fillets and oil are sold in squeeze tubes and jars, imported from Europe. They can be found in delicatessens or the supermarket specialty-food aisle.

ARMAGNAC
Dry brandy, similar to Cognac, distilled in—and made from wine produced in—the Armagnac region of southwestern France. Other good-quality dry wine–based brandies may be substituted.

AVOCADO
The finest-flavored variety of this popular vegetable-fruit is the Haas, which has a pearlike shape and a thick, bumpy, dark green skin. Ripe, ready-to-use avocados will yield slightly to fingertip pressure.

To remove the pit neatly, first, using a sharp knife, cut down to the pit lengthwise all around the avocado. Gently twist the halves in opposite directions to separate; lift away the half without the pit.

Cup the half with the pit in the palm of one hand, with your fingers and thumb safely clear. Hold a sturdy, sharp knife with the other hand and strike the pit with the blade of the knife, wedging the blade firmly into the pit. Then twist and lift the knife to remove the pit.

BAY LEAVES
Whole, dried leaves of the bay laurel tree. Pungent and spicy, they flavor simmered dishes, marinades and pickling mixtures.

BELGIAN ENDIVE
Leaf vegetable with refreshing, slightly bitter spear-shaped leaves, white to pale yellow green in color, tightly packed in cylindrical heads 4–6 inches (10–15 cm) long. Also known as chicory or witloof.

CAPERS
Small, pickled buds of a bush common to the Mediterranean, used as a flavoring or garnish for a variety of savory dishes. The salty, sharp-tasting brine may also be used as a seasoning.

CARAMELIZE
To cause sugar, or the sugars present in certain foods such as onions, to darken to a golden brown or deep brown and develop a rich flavor through the steady application of heat.

CARDAMOM
Sweet, exotic-tasting spice mainly used in Middle Eastern and Indian cooking and in Scandinavian baking. Its small, round seeds, which come enclosed inside a husklike pod, are best purchased whole, and the seeds ground as needed.

CAYENNE PEPPER
Very hot ground spice derived from the dried cayenne chili pepper.

CELERIAC
Large, knobby root of a species of celery plant, with a crisp texture and fine flavor closely resembling that of the familiar stalks. Choose smaller, younger roots, to be peeled and eaten raw or cooked. Also known as celery root.

CHÈVRE
French term, widely used outside of France as well, for a number of cheeses made from goat's milk. Most chèvres are fresh and creamy, with a distinctively sharp tang; they are sold shaped into small rounds, about 2 inches (5 cm) in diameter, or logs 1–2 inches (2.5–5 cm) in diameter and 4–6 inches (10–15 cm) long. Some chèvres are coated with herb mixtures or with pepper or ash, which mildly flavors them.

CHILI PEPPER
Any of a wide variety of peppers prized for the mild-to-hot spiciness they add as a seasoning. Red, ripe chilies are sold fresh and dried. Fresh green chilies include the mild-to-hot, dark green poblano; the long, mild Anaheim; and the small, fiery jalapeño. When handling any chili, wear kitchen gloves to prevent any cuts or abrasions on your hands from contacting the pepper's volatile oils; wash your hands well with warm, soapy water, and take special care not to touch your eyes or any other sensitive areas.

CHINESE FIVE-SPICE POWDER
Popular Chinese ground savory seasoning, reddish brown in color, usually combining star anise, fennel or aniseed, **cloves,** cinnamon and **Sichuan peppercorns.** Sold in Asian markets and in specialty-food sections of supermarkets.

CHIVES
Mild, sweet herb with a flavor reminiscent of the onion, to which it is related. Although available dried, fresh chives possess the best flavor.

CHOU PASTRY
Moist dough of flour, butter, eggs and water, which puffs up into a light and airy pastry in the oven. Piped into a ball shape and baked, the resulting pastry is fancifully said to resemble a cabbage—*chou,* in French.

CLOVES
Rich and aromatic flower buds used to spice marinades and pickling brines.

COGNAC
Dry spirit distilled from wine and, strictly speaking, produced in the Cognac region of France. Other good-quality dry wine–based brandies may be substituted.

COMTÉ CHEESE
Smooth, firm cheese from the Franche-Comté region of southeastern France, with a sweet, nutty flavor resembling Swiss **Gruyère.**

CRAB MEAT, COOKED
Already-cooked crab meat is widely available in fish markets or the seafood counters of supermarkets. Most often, it will be frozen; for best flavor and texture, seek out fresh crab meat.

CREAM, HEAVY
Heavy cream, also called double cream, with a high butterfat content—37.6 percent—that adds richness to dips and spreads. It also whips up very well, doubling in volume, although care must be taken not to overwhip the cream, resulting in butter. Avoid long-lasting ultrapasteurized cream, which does not whip well.

CUMIN
Middle Eastern spice with a strong, dusky, aromatic flavor, popular in cuisines of its region of origin along with those of Latin America, India and parts of Europe. Sold either as whole, small, crescent-shaped seeds, or ground.

CURRANTS, DRIED
Produced from a small variety of grapes, these dried fruits resemble tiny raisins but have a stronger, tarter flavor. Sold in the supermarket baking section. If they are unavailable, substitute raisins.

DILL
Herb with fine, feathery leaves and sweet, aromatic flavor well suited to pickling brines, vegetables, seafood, chicken, veal and pork. Sold fresh or dried.

EGGPLANT
Vegetable-fruit with tender, mildly earthy, sweet flesh; a featured ingredient in the classic French ratatouille and in Middle Eastern hors d'oeuvres and appetizers. Also known as aubergines, their shiny skins vary in color from purple to red and from yellow to white, and their shapes range from small and oval to long and slender to large and pear-shaped. The most common variety is large, purple and globular; but slender, purple Asian eggplants, more tender and with fewer, smaller seeds, are available with increasing frequency in supermarkets.

EMMENTHALER
Variety of Swiss cheese with a firm, smooth texture; large holes; and a mellow, slightly sweet and nutty flavor.

FILO
Tissue-thin sheets of flour-and-water pastry used throughout the Middle East as crisp wrappers for savory or sweet fillings. Usually found in the supermarket frozen-food section, or purchased fresh in Middle Eastern delicatessens; defrost frozen filo thoroughly before use. The fragile sheets, which generally measure 10 by 14 inches (25 by 35 cm), must be separated and handled carefully to avoid tearing. As you work with the filo, keep the unused sheets covered with a lightly dampened towel to keep them from drying out. The name derives from the Greek word for *leaf.*

FISH SAUCE
Popular Southeast Asian seasoning prepared from salted, fermented fish, usually anchovies. Available in Asian markets and supermarket specialty-food sections. Known variously as *nuoc mam* (Vietnamese), *nam pla* (Thai) and *patis* (Filipino).

GARAM MASALA
A common Indian household seasoning blend that differs from region to region but which may include such dried ground spices as **cloves, cardamom,** cinnamon, coriander, **cumin,** fennel, fenugreek, **ginger** and **turmeric.** Available in Indian markets and in the spice or specialty-food sections of well-stocked supermarkets.

GELATIN
Unflavored commercial gelatin gives delicate body to hors d'oeuvre mousses. Sold in ¼-oz (7-g) envelopes, each of which is sufficient to jell about 2 cups (500 ml) of liquid.

GINGER
The root of the tropical ginger plant, which yields a sweet, strong-flavored spice. The whole root may be purchased fresh in a supermarket produce department. Dried and ground ginger is commonly available in jars or tins in the spice section.

GOAT CHEESE
See Chèvre.

GORGONZOLA
Italian variety of tangy, creamy, blue-veined cheese. Other creamy blue cheeses may be substituted.

GRUYÈRE
Variety of Swiss cheese with a firm, smooth texture, small holes and a strong, tangy flavor.

LEEK

Sweet, moderately flavored member of the onion family, long and cylindrical in shape with a pale white root end and dark green leaves. Select firm, unblemished leeks, small to medium in size. Grown in sandy soil, leeks require thorough cleaning.

Trim off the tough ends of the dark green leaves. Starting about 1 inch (2.5 cm) from the root end, slit the leek lengthwise. Trim off the roots.

Vigorously swish the leek in a basin or sink filled with cold water. Drain and rinse again; check to make sure that no dirt remains between the tightly packed pale portion of the leaves.

MASCARPONE
Thick, tangy, almost-liquid Italian cream cheese, similar to French crème fraîche.

MUSCAT
Sweet, fragrant, distinctively spicy wine made from the grape variety of the same name.

MUSSELS

The popular, bluish black–shelled bivalves require special cleaning before cooking to remove any dirt adhering to their shells and to remove their "beards"—the fibrous threads by which the mussels connect to rocks or piers in the coastal waters where they grow.

Rinse the mussels thoroughly under cold running water. One at a time, hold them under the water and scrub with a firm-bristled brush to remove any stubborn dirt.

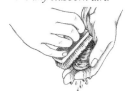

Firmly grasp the fibrous beard attached to the side of each mussel and pull it off. Check all the mussels carefully, discarding those whose shells are not tightly closed.

OLIVE OIL
Extra-virgin olive oil, extracted from olives on the first pressing without the use of heat or chemicals, is preferable. Be sure to choose olive oil that is labeled "extra-virgin." Many brands are now widely available, varying in color and strength of flavor; choose one that suits your taste. Store in an airtight container away from heat and light.

OLIVES, BLACK
Throughout Mediterranean Europe, black olives are cured in various combinations of salt, seasonings, brines, vinegars and oils to produce a range of pungently flavored results that are popular as hors d'oeuvres and appetizers. Good-quality cured olives are available in ethnic delicatessens and well-stocked supermarkets. Olive paste, an imported purée of black olives used as a flavoring ingredient, is packed in jars and squeeze tubes, and sold in delicatessens and specialty-food stores.

ORANGE BLOSSOM HONEY
Widely available commercial honey with a sweet, mild flavor and fragrance reminiscent of the blossoms from whose nectar it is produced.

PAPRIKA
Powdered spice derived from the dried paprika pepper; popular in several European cuisines and available in sweet, mild and hot forms. Hungarian paprika is the best, but Spanish paprika, which is mild, may be used.

PARSLEY
This popular fresh herb is available in two varieties, the more popular curly-leaf type and a flat-leaf type. The latter, also known as Italian parsley, has a more pronounced flavor and is preferred.

PEANUT OIL
All-purpose oil derived from peanuts, for use in dressings and marinades and for sautéing and deep-frying. It may be heated to high temperatures without smoking, which makes it particularly suitable for deep-frying. Vegetable oil also may be used in recipes that call for deep-frying.

PEPPERCORNS
Pepper, the most common of all savory spices, is best purchased as whole peppercorns, to be ground in a pepper mill as needed, or coarsely crushed. Pungent black peppercorns derive from slightly underripe pepper berries, whose hulls oxidize as they dry. Milder white peppercorns come from fully ripened berries, with the husks removed before drying. Sharp-tasting unripened green peppercorns are sold in water, pickled in brine or dried. Spicy pink peppercorns are somewhat similar in shape and flavor, but come from an entirely different plant species, to which some people are allergic; they should be used with caution.

PINE NUTS
Small, ivory-colored seeds extracted from the cones of a species of pine tree, with a rich, slightly resinous flavor. Used whole as an ingredient or garnish, or puréed as a thickener. Also known by the Italian *pinoli*.

PORCINI
Widely used Italian term for *Boletus edulis,* a popular wild mushroom with a rich, meaty flavor. Most commonly sold in dried form, in Italian delicatessens and specialty-food shops, to be reconstituted in liquid as a flavoring for sauces, soups, stews and stuffings. Also known by the French *cèpes.*

RICOTTA
Very light Italian curd cheese made from twice-cooked milk—

traditionally sheep's milk, although cow's milk ricotta is far more common. Ricotta made from partly skimmed milk most closely resembles the Italian product.

ROQUEFORT
French blue-veined cheese made from sheep's milk, with a creamy texture and a rich, sharply tangy flavor. Other creamy blue-veined cheeses may be substituted if necessary.

ROTARY GRATER
Hinged, hand-held device with a hand-turned drum that quickly and neatly grates or shreds nuts, cheeses and other ingredients.

SALMON
Richly flavored and textured, salmon is one of the most popular featured ingredients for hors d'oeuvres and appetizers. Whole fresh fillets may be home-cured to make the popular Scandinavian appetizer known as *gravlax*. Smoked salmon is excellent served on its own, or as an ingredient or embellishment in other recipes; purchase it freshly sliced from a good-quality delicatessen. Lox, which is a salt-cured salmon, and Nova, which is a cold-smoked salmon, are commonly sold in Jewish delicatessens; they have oilier textures and in most cases are not acceptable substitutes for smoked salmon.

SALMON ROE
Bright orange salmon eggs may be served like caviar, with toast or blini and garnishes of

chopped sweet onion or chives, chopped egg and sour cream. They may also be used in spreads or as a garnish for other seafood-based hors d'oeuvres or appetizers. More reasonably priced than caviar, the eggs are generally sold in jars in specialty-food stores or well-stocked supermarkets.

SALT, COARSE OR KOSHER
Coarse-grained salt, sold in the seasonings section of the supermarket, is frequently used in marinades and seasonings. **Sea salt** is an acceptable substitute.

SALT, SEA
Salt extracted by evaporation from sea water has a stronger, more pronounced flavor than regular table salt. Available in coarse and fine grinds in well-stocked supermarkets. The large crystals may be used in place of **coarse or kosher salt.**

SESAME SEEDS
Small, pale ivory-colored seeds with a mild, nutty flavor; used as an ingredient or garnish in hors d'oeuvres and appetizers.

SICHUAN PEPPERCORNS
Chinese spice whose hollow, brown berries resemble common black peppercorns but have a less sharp—although no less aromatic—flavor.

SORREL
Fresh herb resembling in shape and color a small, pale variety of spinach, with a mild, refresh-ingly acidic flavor. Available in well-stocked supermarkets.

SUMMER SAVORY
Delicate green herb that complements the flavors of vegetables, seafood and poultry. Best in its fresh form, although also widely available dried.

SWEET PEPPERS (CAPSICUMS)
Fresh, sweet-fleshed members of the pepper family, of which the most common is the bell pepper, named for its generous, curved shape. Bell peppers are readily available in their unripe green form, athough ripened red or yellow bell peppers are also available. Creamy pale yellow, orange and purple black types may also be found. Other varieties of sweet peppers include bull's horn, Cuban and pimiento.

TARAMA
The small pink eggs, or roe, of the gray mullet or cod, the principal ingredient in the Greek hors d'oeuvre spread known as taramasalata. Salted and packed in jars or available in bulk, the eggs are sold in Greek and Middle Eastern markets or well-stocked supermarkets.

TARTLET PAN
Metal pan, usually of tinned steel, containing shallow, sometimes fluted, circular impressions, about 1–2¾ inches (2.5–7 cm) across, for shaping and baking tartlets.

TOMATOES
Of the many forms of tomatoes available, small, round, bite-sized cherry tomatoes are the ones most commonly used as hors d'oeuvres. Medium plum tomatoes (also called egg or Roma tomatoes) provide attractive, small slices for first-course presentations and are also excellent in sauces. When good-

quality, sun-ripened tomatoes are not in season, use canned imported Italian tomatoes for making sauces.

TROUT, SMOKED
Sold in specialty-food stores and delicatessens, smoked trout has a mild, sweet flavor and moist,, tender texture that make it an excellent ingredient for hors d'oeuvres and appetizers.

TURMERIC
Pungent, earthy-flavored ground spice that, like saffron, adds a vibrant yellow color to any dish.

VERMOUTH
Dry or sweet wine commercially enhanced with herbs and barks to give it an aromatic flavor.

VINEGAR
Literally "sour" wine, vinegar results when certain strains of yeast cause wine—or some other alcoholic liquid—to ferment for a second time, turning it acidic. The best-quality wine vinegars begin with good-quality wines, whether red or white. Asian rice vinegar, made from rice wine, has a sweet, mild flavor.

YEAST, ACTIVE DRY
The most widely available form of yeast for baking, commonly sold in individual 1-tablespoon (¼-oz/7-g) packages and found in the baking section of the supermarket. Seek out one of the new strains of fast-acting yeast available in specialty-food stores.

ZEST
Thin, brightly colored, outer-most layer of a citrus fruit's peel, containing most of its aromatic oils. A lively source of flavor, zest may be removed with a simple tool known as a zester, with a hand-held grater or with a vegetable peeler or paring knife.

Index

ACKNOWLEDGMENTS

The publishers would like to thank the following people and organizations for
their generous assistance and support in producing this book:
Janique Poncelet, Ruth Jacobson, Jane Fraser, Amy Morton, Ken DellaPenta,
Rapid Lasergraphics (San Francisco), Danielle di Salvo, Maria Antonis, Stephen Griswold,
John Powell, the buyers for Gardener's Eden, and the buyers and store managers for
Williams-Sonoma and Pottery Barn stores.

The following kindly lent props for the photography:
Stephanie Greenleigh, Sue Fisher King, Lorraine & Judson Puckett, Gianfranco Salvio,
Sue White and Chuck Williams.